THE PEACHTREE
GARDEN BOOK

THE PEACHTREE

GARDEN
BOOK

GARDENING IN THE SOUTHEAST

EDITED BY

EDITH HENDERSON, Fellow
American Society of Landscape Architects

WRITERS

OLIVE ROBINSON
CALLIE EFIRD
EDITH HENDERSON

A PROJECT OF

THE PEACHTREE GARDEN CLUB
ATLANTA, GEORGIA

Member of

The Garden Club of America, Inc.
The Garden Club of Georgia, Inc.
The National Council of State Garden Clubs

CHAMBERS AND ASHER BOOKS

RESEARCH

Cary Lide — Vegetable Gardening

SOURCES

Dr. Woolford Baker — Professor Emeritus, Emory University
Mr. Elbridge Freeborn — Horticulturist, Writer
Mr. Erik A. Johnson — Horticulturist, Plantsman
Mr. Frank A. Smith — Horticulturist, Plantsman
Donald Hastings, Sr. — Horticulturist, Plantsman
Donald Hastings, Jr. — Horticulturist, Plantsman

Cover and book design: Chuck Clemens
Diagrams through the courtesy of
White Flower Farm, Litchfield, Connecticut 06759
Eliot Wadsworth II, President
Illustrations: The Iconographic Encyclopedia of Science, Literature and Art.
    1851 Edition.
Typesetting: Alice Teeter and Bea Connor
Layout by: Tommy Westbrook

First Edition: 1926
Second Edition: 1956
Third Edition: 1982
Fourth Edition: 1988

Chambers and Asher Books
1776 Nancy Creek Bluff, N.W.
Atlanta, Georgia 30327

For additional copies call
404-876-8761 or write
Peachtree Publishers
Armour Circle, N.E.
Atlanta, Georgia 30324

FOREWORD

In 1926 the Peachtree Garden Club published the Garden Schedule, ghost written every step of the way by the Club's finest. It was accurate, informative and helpful.

Forty years later, guided by a rich heritage of incomparable know-how, we published its second edition entitled "The Peachtree Planner."

Fifty-six years later, a third edition, "The Peachtree Garden Book" is here. It will inform, delight and guide all who watch seeds sprout, flowers grow, shrubs bloom and trees mature. Design ideas are helpful, insect sprays lose their mystery, and vegetables will produce. Prepare to enjoy!

Edith Henderson, Editor

Edith Henderson is a practicing Landscape Architect in Atlanta, Georgia. She is a Fellow of the American Society of Landscape Architects. She is the first woman to have served as Chair of the Council of Fellows.

5

CONTENTS

Forward 5

CHAPTER I

THE CALENDAR

Month By Month
Guide to the Garden

Map. 8
January. 10
February 12
March 15
April 18
May. 21
June 24
July 27
August 30
September. 33
October. 35
November. 38
December 41

CHAPTER II

LANDSCAPE DESIGN

Foundation Planning. 43
The Patio 44
Entrances and Exits 44

CHAPTER III

HOW TO PREPARE AND MAINTAIN THE SOUTHEASTERN GARDEN

Soil Preparation Fertilizer
and Mulch 45
Planting, Transplanting
and Grubbing Out 48
Watering 52
Pest and Disease Control . 53
Tools 56

CHAPTER IV

WHAT TO PLANT AND HOW TO PLANT IT IN THE SOUTHEAST

Southern Lawns 57
Ground Covers. 59
Vines 60
Trees 62
Shrubs. 64
Shrubs of Special Interest
in the Southeast 68
    Hollies. 68
    Azaleas 70
    Camellias 73
    Roses. 75
Wildflowers and Ferns . . .76
Bulbous Flowers 80
The Flower Border 83
    Annuals 83
    Biennials 85
    Perennials 86
Cut Flowers 87
Drying Flowers. 88
Vegetables. 90
Herbs 92

GLOSSARY

For the Working Gardener 94

MAP OF THE SOUTHERN PIEDMONT AREA

THE CALENDAR

Mother Nature is very lenient with us as to temperatures in the South. There are almost always ten months of bloom, from early jonquils in February to the last straggling chrysanthemums of December. The sun is fierce enough to make summer gardening apathetic, but the long autumns give three months good planting time. The two coldest months have sunshine enough for jasmine nudiflorum and lonicera fragrantissima to break into winter bloom. The berried shrubs hold their berries the winter through, while our broadleaved evergreens *are* evergreen. The open winters make it uncongenial for lilacs and the shrubs that need hard cold to force their spring resurrection; still, month by month, there is work and joy in the garden.

Starting in the early '80's, we have experienced several severe winters, causing most experts to *partially* classify the area in Zone 7 in hardiness rather than in Zone 8.

Timing in the monthly gardening calendar is based on average weather and soil conditions for the Southeast area. The region is known as the Southern Piedmont. It includes Alabama, Georgia, North Carolina, South Carolina, and Virginia. In this large area there is little difference in climate.

JANUARY

THE MONTH FOR PLANNING

WEATHER AND SOIL

After freezes check beds for heaving. Be sure to check mulch on tender plants; use leaves and pine needles. Brush or shake off heavy snow before it freezes; do not try to remove ice from branches. If salt is used on drive, remove salted snow from any plants.

FLOWERS

Annuals: During mild spell sow hardy annuals such as sweet peas, larkspur and corn flowers. Sow other annuals in cold frame or indoors.

Perennials: Can be moved if ground is not frozen. Never cover cold-loving plants such as peonies and tritomas.

VEGETABLES

Plan; order seed; try something new. Apply lime (except to Irish potato bed). Apply well rotted manure.

Plant hardy English peas outdoors in late January.

Start seeds such as broccoli, cabbage, collards and onions indoors for planting outdoors in March.

SHRUBS

All shrubs may be moved or newly planted now during dormant period. No shrub pruning necessary but can be done.

Check mulch on tender shrubs and pull away from trunks.

Make cuttings from deciduous plants.

TREES

All deciduous trees can be pruned when dormant if needed.

Needle-like trees can also be pruned during cold season if needed.

LAWNS

If lawn is thin, use processed manure.

FERTILIZERS

Dress whole garden with humus (compost or rotted manure), especially areas to be planted in March.

INSECT AND DISEASE CONTROL

Plant something for the birds so that they will stay and eat your bugs next summer.

PLAN AHEAD

Study catalogues for seeds, plants and equipment. Make changes in garden and entire lot on paper. Check operating order of all equipment.

BLOOMS

FLOWERS	SHRUBS	BERRIES
Bloodroot	Camellia	Aucuba
Christmas Rose	Daphne	Barberry
Early Small Jonquil	January Jasmine	Callicarpa
Lenten Rose	Tea Olive	Dogwood
	Wintersweet	Euonymus
	Witchhazel	Holly
	Christmas Honeysuckle	Mahonia
		Nandina
		Photinia
		Pyracantha

MISCELLANEOUS

Force branches of early flowering shrubs in fresh water in a sunny window.

Don't forget to feed the birds!

FEBRUARY

THE MONTH FOR PRUNING

WEATHER AND SOIL

Hard freezes are still to be expected. During open weather, get beds ready for planting by deep spading. Add humus, sand, manure, and fertilizers to soil as needed. Be sure soil is dry enough to work.

FLOWERS

Annuals: Start hardy flower seeds late in the month.

Perennials: Can be moved now.

Set out pansies and violas.

Roses: Plant, prune, move.

VEGETABLES

Repair the ground; deep spade, lime, turn leaves and manure according to need.

Early February: Start hardy seeds indoors (broccoli, Brussels sprouts, cauliflower, onions, parsley).

Plant early English peas out as soon as possible.

Late February: If the weather breaks, plant Irish potatoes, onion sets, garlic, asparagus, Brussels sprouts, and lettuce plants.

Start tender plants of tomatoes, peppers, and eggplant indoors.

SHRUBS

Deciduous: Can be planted.

Broadleaf evergreens: Can be planted. Prune newly planted boxwood; prune other shrubs before new growth starts, if shaping is needed.

Needle-like: Do not prune now.

Flowering: Current season budding shrubs should be pruned now. Cut out dead wood of all flowering shrubs. Cut hydrangeas back ¾ of growth.

TREES

Plant dogwoods, evergreens, and shade trees.

Prune fruit trees; prune crape myrtle, if desired.

LAWNS

Start re-seeding tired and dead spots in old lawns.

Use chickweed killer where necessary to control winter weeds.

FERTILIZERS

Feed broadleaf evergreens.

Feed flowering shrubs.

INSECT AND DISEASE CONTROL

If temperature is above 40°, use dormant spray of Volck oil or lime sulphur on ornamentals that are susceptible to insect and scale damage.

Use pre-emergence crabgrass killer on lawns, and dig out wild onions.

Paint scraps of board yellow, coat with the thickest engine oil available, and place in the greenhouse among white fly infested plants. It works like fly paper.

PLAN AHEAD

Get ready for next month's frantic pace!

BLOOMS

FLOWERS
Crocus
Early Hyacinth
Early Jonquil
Snowdrop
Violet
Wall Flower

SHRUBS
Flowering Almond
Baby's Breath Spirea
Camellia
Forsythia
January Jasmine
Flowering Quince
Viburnum Tinus

MISCELLANEOUS

Feed the birds.

MARCH

THE MONTH FOR DIGGING

WEATHER AND SOIL

March can be very cold or deceivingly warm. Start working on soil the minute it dries out. Mulch borders. Work beds for next month's seeds. Turn compost. Start removing mulch from bulbs and slowly from rock gardens.

FLOWERS

Annuals: Regardless of beautiful weather, DO NOT PLANT SEEDS IN OPEN GROUND NOW. Sow summer annuals in coldframe.

Thin and transplant fall-sown annuals (larkspur, corn-flowers, calliopsis).

Perennials: Divide as they come up.
Move wildflowers.
Plant clematis and other vines.
Prune ivy.

Roses: Prune, fertilize, apply systemic insecticide and mulch.

Biennials: In this Southeastern area expect foxglove, Sweet William, and hollyhock to act like perennials, because they re-seed themselves most of the time.

VEGETABLES

If February weather was difficult, begin now.

Plant seed of turnips, mustard, collards, carrots, beets, celery, and lettuce in Mid-March.

Prepare soil for summer garden.

Do not work the soil if too wet.

SHRUBS

Broadleaf evergreens: Balled and burlapped plants still can be set out.

Flowering: Small plants that are bareroot can still be set.

Prune after flowering if shrub flowers on old wood.

Prune before flowering if shrub flowers on current season wood.

TREES

Earliest to color: Weeping Willow (pale green), Purple leaf plum (pale pink), Bradford pear (white), Yoshino cherry (blush pink).

LAWNS

Apply pre-emergence crabgrass killer.

Mow lawns overplanted with rye at 1″.

Fertilize new lawns. It is not too early to start perennial grasses if sown in dry soil.

FERTILIZERS

Feed azaleas and camellias immediately after bloom.

Feed flowering shrubs and pyracantha if not fed previously.

Feed fall sown annuals with light application of balanced fertilizer.

Feed bulbs immediately after blooming.

INSECT AND DISEASE CONTROL

Slugs: Trap with beer, or overturned grapefruit rinds, or sprinkle slugs with salt. Any rough material, like sharp sand or screening around plants, is a deterrent.

Moles: Plant Caper Spurge or Euphorbia lathrus.

To prevent damping off of seedlings, drench soil with camomile tea.

PLAN AHEAD

Order new chrysanthemums and hardy asters.

BLOOMS

FLOWERS
Alyssum Saxatile
Crocus
Daisy
Hyacinth
Narcissus
Pansy
Early Tulip
Violet
Wall Flower
Snowdrop

SHRUBS
Deciduous Azalea
Baby's Breath Spirea
Chinese Magnolia
Crabapple
Exochorda
Forsythia
Loropetalum
Flowering Quince

TREES
Acer Rubrum
Buckeye
Catalpa
Cherry
Hybrid Crabapple
Japanese Magnolia
Magnolia Glauca
    (Southern Sweetbay)
Pear
Purple Leaf Plum
Redbud

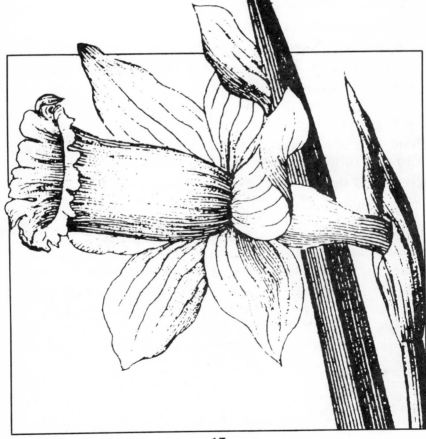

APRIL

THE MONTH FOR SOWING

WEATHER AND SOIL

Most cautious gardeners wait until either April 15 or Easter Monday to plant tender seeds and plants outdoors. The soil is easy to cultivate and not yet heat-hardened.

FLOWERS

Annuals: After 15th, sow annuals in open ground.

Transplant seedlings.

Plant pots for the terrace.

Keep pansies picked.

Perennials: Can be divided still if clumps are not too advanced.

Roses: Plant new. Remove earth mounds from roses after frost. Fertilize late April.

Plant summer-flowering bulbs such as gladioli, ismenes, tritomas, tube-roses, funkias, etc., every two weeks.

Keep dead flowers picked off of blooming bulbs.

Start caladiums in pots.

VEGETABLES

Early April: Fertilize late winter planted vegetables. Continue planting lettuce, beets, carrots, onions, etc.

After danger of frost, plant all Summer vegetables except okra, cowpeas, sweet potatoes, pumpkin, and eggplant.

AFTER FROST	LATE APRIL
Bush beans	Lima beans
Pole beans	All squash
Roasting ear corn	Cucumbers
Summer greens	Cantaloupe
Summer Bibb lettuce	Watermelon
Swiss Chard	Tomatoes
	Sweet corn

18

SHRUBS

Prune hedges now, if necessary.

Broadleaf evergreen: If you must prune, do it very lightly.

Flowering: Prune after bloom, if buds set on new growth.

LAWNS

It is not too late to start new cool weather lawns and renovate old. Sweep and top-dress old lawn with sifted topsoil, then fertilize. Dethatch Bermuda, zoysia, and centipede.

FERTILIZERS

Feed azaleas after bloom.

Make time schedule for feeding everything in garden. Be sure all plants are fed before hot weather.

Feed magnolia grandiflora with well-rotted cow manure. (This will last all year.)

INSECT AND DISEASE CONTROL

Spray onion water to temporarily deter aphids, white flies, mealy bugs and spider mites. Import ladybugs as a predator!

Use solution of ground hot peppers for fleas and caterpillars.

Crushed eggshells and firefly larvae deter cutworms.

Pyrethrin sprays can control aphids, leaf hoppers, and household pests, if used repeatedly.

PLAN AHEAD

Start ordering perennial seed for planting in July.

Check supply of compost and mulch for summer protection.

BLOOMS

FLOWERS
Alyssum
Virginia Bluebells
Columbine
Hyacinth
Dwarf Iris
Phlox Subulata
Pink
Primrose
Ranunculus
Scilla
Star of Bethlehem
Thrift
Tulip
Wisteria

SHRUBS
Almond
Azalea
Deutzia
Kerria
Lilac
Mock Orange
Pearl Bush
Photina
Pittosporum
Banksia Rose
Rugosa Rose
Scotch Broom
Spirea
Sweet Shrub
Weigela

TREES
Dogwood
Flowering Cherry
Fringe Tree
Halesia (Silverbell)
Hawthorne
Mimosa
Pear
Redbud
Serviceberry
Stewartia

VINES
Caroling Yellow Jessamine
Clematis

MAY

THE MONTH FOR BLOOMING

WEATHER AND SOIL

Working conditions are still pleasant, but it's sometimes wet, sometimes hot. If wet, check for rot, mildew and other problems caused by poor drainage.

Start controlling weeds.

FLOWERS

Stake all tall plants and tie up trailing vines.

Annuals: Set bedding plants and sow seed early in the month.

Start succession of hot weather annuals such as zinnias, marigolds, celosia, portulaca.

Pinch back petunias, sweet alyssum and ageratum.

Keep pansies picked.

Perennials: Set out rooted chrysanthemum cuttings and pinch back cushion chrysanthemums.

Sow dwarf dahlias and plant dahlia tubers at end of month. Note: Plant stakes first.

Plant more gladioli.

Plant dwarf perennials, such as dwarf coreopsis, as edgings.

VEGETABLES

When ground temperature is 70° plant:

okra (soak seeds 24 hours)
pumpkin
sweet potato slips
eggplant
pepper plants
peanuts
watermelon
cow peas
butter peas
black-eyed peas
crowder peas
butter beans

Second crop
lima beans
bush beans
sweet corn

Water only when necessary.

Thinly spread hay is a good mulch.

Control flea beetles, worms, and aphids with Diazinon or malathion, dipel dust, or thuricide spray.

SHRUBS

Transplant small wild azalea while in bloom. Mark larger ones for fall moving.

LAWNS

It is too late to start Fescues and perennial grasses such as Kentucky Bluegrass.

It is not too late to start summer grasses such as Hulled or Hybrid Bermuda, Centipede and Meyer or Matrella Zoysia.

FERTILIZERS

If soil is excessively wet, do not fertilize.

Feed roses to get second bloom.

Feed later blooming azaleas after bloom.

Feed March vegetables with 10-10-10.

INSECT AND DISEASE CONTROL

To repel deer: Deposit human hair in the garden and plant foxgloves.

Hot salty water will kill weeds.

Praying Mantis feed on flies, grasshoppers, locusts, wasps, and caterpillars.

Use manure tea spray for Black Spot on roses.

PLAN AHEAD

Order perennial seed for July if not already ordered.

Make arrangements for vacation time care of your garden.

BLOOMS

FLOWERS		SHRUBS	TREES
Ajuga	Lily	Azaleas	Cherry
Anchusa	Painted Daisy	Beauty Bush	Magnolia Grandiflora
Anthemis	Peony	Deutzia	Cucumber Tree
Aster Alpinus	Phlox Divaricata	Gardenia	(Magnolia Acuminata)
Bleeding Heart	Pink	Florida Jasmine	Umbrella Magnolia
Campanula	Poppy	Kerria	(Magnolia Tripetala)
Candytuft	Primrose	Lilac	Sourwood
Clematis	Rose	Mountain Laurel	
Columbine	Salvia	St. Johnswort	BULBS
Cornflower	Snapdragon	Scotch Broom	Caladium
Delphinium	Sweet Pea	Spirea	Peruvian Daffodil
Begonia	Sweet William	Weigela	Camassia
Foxglove	Thrift		Tuberose
Geum	Late Tulip		
Hemerocallis			VINES
Iris			Climbing Hydrangea
Impatiens			Confederate Jasmine

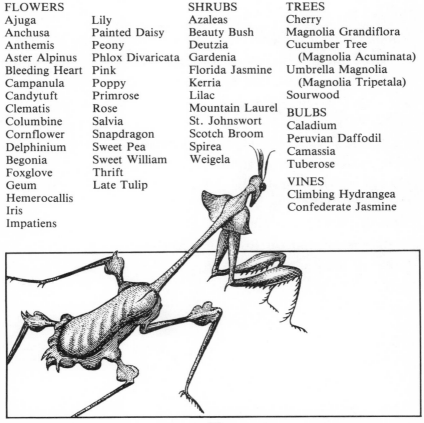

JUNE

THE MONTH FOR SPRAYING

WEATHER AND SOIL

Hot weather has come! June-September is normally the driest season. Water everything as it needs it; do not let hard soil dry out; to prevent loss by evaporation, water after midday. Water window boxes, hanging baskets and most potted plants daily. Be sure garden beds are well conditioned with peat, humus and/or vermiculite and that all widely spread plantings and moisture-loving shrubs are well mulched.

FLOWERS

Annuals: Pinch back to make bushy and feed moderately.

Set new plants to replenish borders.

Keep sowing hot weather annuals for succession of bloom.

Perennials: If over-planting, cut out yellowed foliage of spring bulbs.

Dig tulips, dry several days, store till fall.

Pinch back chrysanthemums.

Last chance to plant dahlias, tuberoses, tigridias, cannas and gladioli by mid-month.

Cut back bearded iris and divide. Keep Japanese iris watered.

Take stem cuttings of tuberous begonias.

Roses: Prune ramblers.

VEGETABLES

Pull spent plants.

Re-till soil.

Plant second crops.

Water well, but only when needed.

Check for need of insect control and fungus control sprays.

SHRUBS

Deciduous and broadleaf evergreen: Take cuttings for rooting in sand or vermiculite. Use air-layering method on hard to root plants.

Flowering: Take cuttings of azaleas now. They should be rooted by the end of August.

TREES

Deep water all young trees set out for less than 2 years.

Check pines and dogwood for borers.

Spray or paint pines with a Chlordane solution.

Prune arborvitaes, junipers, yews and hemlocks in June, since they have completed their main growth for the season. This creates good structure.

LAWNS

Use weed killer only if temperature is above 70°.

Plant ground covers where grass won't grow.

FERTILIZERS

Feed Gumpo azaleas after bloom.

Last chance to feed camellias and broadleaf evergreens.

Continue feeding roses and chrysanthemums on schedule.

If fertilizing or mulching with manure in dry season, be sure the manure is very old.

INSECT AND DISEASE CONTROL

Tobacco dust mixed with mulch prevents tomato wilt.

Steamed bone meal deters ants.

If insect pests are a major problem in a flower bed or vegetable garden, plan a different crop in the area next year.

PLAN AHEAD

Order bulbs for fall planting.

Get flats and seed beds ready for July perennial seed.

BLOOMS

FLOWERS
Anthemis	Hollyhock	Poppy
Begonia	Hydrangea	Roses
Campanula	Impatiens	Salvia
Celosia	Japanese Iris	Shasta Daisy
Crinum Lily	Larkspur	Snapdragon
Delphinium	Madonna Lily	Stokesia
Foxglove	Marigold	Sweet Pea
Gaillardia	Pansy	Sweet William
Geranium	Petunia	Tritoma
Hemerocallis	Phlox	Veronica
	Pinks	

SHRUBS
Abelia
Mountain Laurel
St. Johnswort

TREES
Goldenrain Tree
Magnolia
Mimosa
Sourwood

VINES
Clematis
Climbing Hydrangea
Confederate Jasmine

JULY

THE MONTH FOR HOEING

WEATHER AND SOIL

Whether watering or not, a crust should not be allowed to form around plants. Be sure to mulch beds not thickly planted. Depend on working and mulching to conserve moisture. If watering must be done, do it thoroughly by soaking instead of spraying.

FLOWERS

Be sure all tall plants are securely staked.

Annuals: Replace spent perennials with annuals.

Last chance to set out zinnias, petunias, and fast bloomers for fall bloom.

When pulling up poppies, cornflowers and larkspur, shake seed where you want them next year.

Perennials: Sow perennial seed for next spring's bloom; sow seed in good loam, plus a third more sand and place in partial shade.

Continue pinching chrysanthemums and dahlias.

Plant new and divide old bearded iris.

Dig and dry out jonquil bulbs.

Cut back wisteria to encourage next year's bloom.

Roses: Rest plants; do not feed or overwater, but keep spraying; prune lightly to encourage new fall growth.

VEGETABLES

Remove tomato suckers and root them for new plants.

Dig Irish potatoes when leaves yellow.

Spray vegetables regularly to control insects, rot, mildew, and worms.

Fertilize vegetables every 4 to 6 weeks.

Start seed for September 1 planting:

Broccoli	Cauliflower
Brussels Sprouts	Collards
Cabbage	Onions

SHRUBS

Deciduous and broadleaf evergreens: Check mulch and keep watered.

Flowering: Good time to graft azaleas and camellias.
Remove faded flowers from crape myrtles for rebloom.
Buddleia is at its height now, also vitex.
Prune hydrangeas after bloom.

TREES

Continue watering trees less than two years old.

LAWNS

Raise blade on mower to 2″.

Bermuda grass thrives in hot weather, so plant hulled Bermuda seed or sprigs of Tift Bermuda in thin places.

FERTILIZERS

Last chance to feed azaleas and camellias.

Do not feed roses, only soak.

Continue regular schedules for garden flowers.

INSECT AND DISEASE CONTROL

Firefly adults are predators of snails and slugs.

Many fungus diseases can be stopped by applying a horse-radish spray.

Mint leaves around plants ward off rodents.

PLAN AHEAD

Order fall bulbs.

BLOOMS

FLOWERS			SHRUBS
Asclepias	Helianthus	Roses	Abelia
Aster	Hemerocallis	Snapdragon	Buddleia
Calliopsis	Hosta	Stokesia	Crape Myrtle
Celosia	Hydrangea	Tiger Lily	Gardenia
Dahlia	Lantana	Tuberous Begonia	Hydrangea
Gaillardia	Lily	Tuberose	Mallow
Geranium	Marigold	Zinnia	St. Johnswort
Gerbera	Platycodon		
Gladiolus			TREES
			Magnolia
			Mimosa

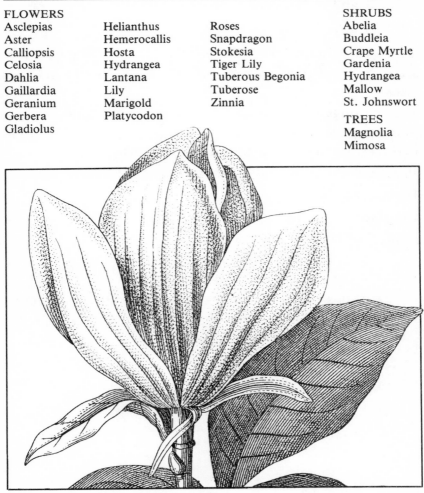

AUGUST

THE MONTH FOR ROOTING

WEATHER AND SOIL

Let the hose run on hot, hard earth for hours. Do not sprinkle. Follow with heavy mulch. The state agriculture experiment station is not pushed now; send soil samples for analysis and recommendation (see SOIL).

FLOWERS

Keep dead blooms off of all plants; keep weeding borders.

Annuals: Still time to sow portulaca; it flowers in three weeks.

Take cuttings of snapdragons, carnations and phlox.

Perennials: Sow pansy seed. Also sow English daisies, columbines, gerberas, shasta daisies, veronicas.

Prick out earlier seedlings where two true leaves appear.

Divide Japanese iris.

Continue to let roses rest.

Plant freesias for winter in house.

Plant madonna lilies and newer hybrid lilies such as "Mid Century" group and Imperials, Sentinels and Aurelians.

Take cuttings from rock garden plants such as sedum, phlox, and pinks to put in coldframe for winter.

VEGETABLES

Sow cowpeas as summer cover crop in areas open in early August.

Fertilize any vegetable that will produce another crop.

Protect melons from insects and worms with plastic under each.

Spray for disease, rot, fungus.

Dust with Sevin for insects.

Start seed in trays:

Cauliflower
Collards
Broccoli
Cabbage
Onions

Sow bush beans, cucumbers and squash in the ground.

SHRUBS

Flowering: Disbud camellias.

LAWNS

Sow patches in old lawns first, then start winter grasses the last week in August if cool.

FERTILIZERS

Feed chrysanthemums every two weeks with liquid manure until buds appear.

Feed dahlias every two weeks with liquid manure until buds appear, the last feeding when buds begin to show color.

Top dress begonias with dried cow manure.

INSECT AND DISEASE CONTROL

If mildew has "attacked" your zinnias, it is not too late to start a new crop from seed, to enjoy into November.

Dried blood repels rabbits.

White geraniums repel Japanese Beetles.

Dragonflies feed on mosquitos.

PLAN AHEAD

Start planning and ordering shrubs and trees for fall planting.

BLOOMS

FLOWERS

Ageratum
Begonia
Calendula
Celosia
China Aster
Cosmos
Dahlia
Geranium
Gladiolus
Hemerocallis

Impatiens
Liriope
Marigold
Phlox
Rose
Rudbeckia
Snapdragon
Stokesia
Zinnia

SHRUBS

Abelia
Buddleia
Crape Myrtle
Hydrangea
Mallow

VINES

Clematis paniculata
   (Sweet Autumn Clematis)

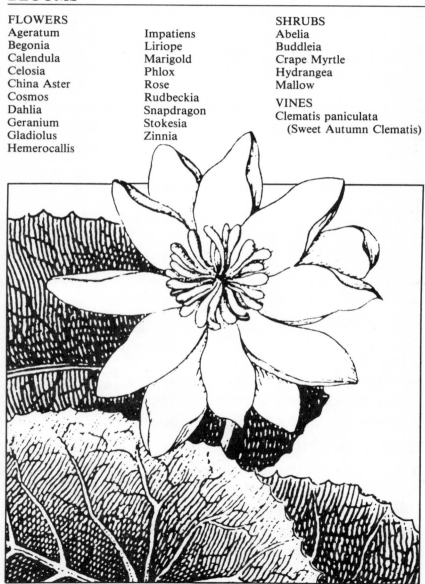

SEPTEMBER

THE MONTH FOR SOWING GRASS SEED

WEATHER AND SOIL

Hot and hard — if not properly worked and mulched!

FLOWERS

Annuals: Cut back scraggly plants for further fall growth.

Perennials: Transplant seedlings from July plantings.

Divide summer-flowering plants such as hostas and hemerocallis.

Divide all irises not cared for in August.

Continue to sow seeds of Sweet William, English daisies, stock, snapdragons.

Plant paperwhites and other bulbs for indoor forcing.

VEGETABLES

Set out plants seeded earlier.

Plant hardy herbs now.

Seed cool weather plants now (i.e. turnips, spinach, beets, carrots, lettuce, etc.)

Sow crimson clover as winter cover crop.

Continue dust and spray program.

SHRUBS

By the end of this month, planting plans for old and new houses can be carried out.

It is not too early to set out container-grown camellias.

LAWNS

Sow winter Rye grass. Try to get it up before the first light frost. Rye is oversown on Bermuda or carpet grasses to insure winter green.

Continue to sow fescues and perennial grasses.

FERTILIZERS

Continue scheduled feeding of dahlias and chrysanthemums with liquid fertilizer.

INSECT AND DISEASE CONTROL

Prepare house plants summered outside to come indoors. Spray with pyrethrin at 2 week intervals to discourage insects.

PLAN AHEAD

Overhaul cold frames for winter seedlings.

Order shrubs and trees to be planted next month.

Order seeds to be sown in October: larkspur, double pink poppies, cornflowers, sweet peas.

Start collecting cones, acorns, dried leaves of cucumber magnolias, etc., for Christmas wreaths and decorations.

BLOOMS

FLOWERS		SHRUBS
Anemone	Four O'clock	Abelia
Aster	Geranium	Buddleia
Begonia	Gladiolus	Camellia
Calendula	Impatiens	
Celosia	Marigold	
Cleome	Rose	
Cosmos	Salvia	
Dahlia	Snapdragon	
Delphinium	Tuberose	
	Zinnia	

OCTOBER

THE MONTH TO DIG, MOVE & DIVIDE

WEATHER AND SOIL

October can be hot or cool. If cool, it is a good month to dig, move and divide plants, re-arrange the garden and prepare soil for next month's heavy planting schedule of flowers, shrubs and bulbs.

FLOWERS

Gather flowers to dry before frost.

Annuals: Sow larkspur and other hardy annuals.

Remove plants from borders.

Perennials: If cool enough, divide and replant where needed.

Plant seedlings in permanent place.

It is safe to plant early flowering Dutch bulbs after first frost.

Cut back gladioli tops and burn.

Take up clumps of caladiums and other summer tubers and bulbs for storing while you can find them.

Mulch bulbs with half-rotted leaves, bone meal and cow manure.

Bring in house plants before frost. Decide whether to take cuttings or winter-over geraniums. Take begonia cuttings for Christmas bloom.

Prepare any special pot plants such as tree lantanas or fuchsias, topiary forms, etc., for winter by moving them inside.

VEGETABLES

Not too late to sow parsley, spinach, turnips, and radishes.

Harvest sweet potatoes before frost.

Plant large onions for next summer, onion sets for this winter.

Sow cover crops (see August, September).

Rye grass can be sown to keep down weeds.

SHRUBS

Consider using anti-dessicants on plants growing out of their native habitat or in an exposed location.

Continue to water well, if dry.

It is safe to plant all shrubs this month.

TREES

Can be planted now.

LAWNS

The first of the month is the last chance to sow Rye grass; it is safer and quicker when planted in September.

Feed lawns for the last time.

Mow last time at 2″ high.

Rake leaves before they mat down.

Test soil. Apply lime if needed.

FERTILIZERS

Well established broadleaf evergreens actually need nothing more than a good mulch for the winter. But, if camellias and broadleaf evergreens are not hardening-off themselves, feed them a fall conditioner fertilizer the last of the month.

Cease feeding roses.

INSECT AND DISEASE CONTROL

Before storing tender bulbs dug up for the winter (caladiums, dahlias, etc.), dust with fungicide.

PLAN AHEAD

Prepare compost: Turn and check, make room for fall debris.

Nursery stock of shrubs and trees is best now. Buy and order what is needed and save for November planting.

BLOOMS

FLOWERS
Anemone
Aster
Celosia
Chrysanthemum
Cosmos
Cleome
Dahlia

Geranium
Marigold
Phlox
Rose
Salvia
Zinnia

SHRUBS
Camellia japonica
Camellia sasanqua
Osmanthus

NOVEMBER

THE MONTH FOR PLANTING

WEATHER AND SOIL

Since November 1st is the average date of the first hard frost, this month is the year's best time for all planting. Check soil for preparation and drainage in order to be ready for planting. Make a general clean-up of the garden the first of the month.

FLOWERS

Annuals: Continue sowing larkspur, cornflowers and other hardy annuals.

Continue planting pansies and English daisies.

Perennials: Cut herbaceous perennials 2″ above ground.

Plant all perennials in permanent places.

Roses: Plant new roses; mound soil around all roses and mulch for winter. Cut out old wood on climbing roses.

Bulb planting is in full swing. If soil is not good, put a handful of sand under tulip bulbs. Do not let bone meal touch any bulbs; work it into soil around planting.

Plant more bulbs for indoor forcing.

Pot up chrysanthemums for indoor bloom.

Biennials: Transplant those rootings taken in late summer.

Start new plants from cuttings set in open ground from pinks, Sweet William, shasta daisies, anthemis, scabiosa, coreopsis, etc.

VEGETABLES

Harvest before hard freeze.

Plant English peas.

Remove all spent plants to prevent insects and disease.

Plant Austrian winter peas as green manure and cover crop while warm enough.

Lime garden if needed.

Start Bibb lettuce indoors in trays.

Tie up berry canes to prevent winter breakage.

SHRUBS

Transplant rooted cuttings to cold frame.

Deciduous: Plant as soon as leaves fall.

Broadleaf evergreens: Planting in full swing.

Flowering: Plant ornamentals.

TREES

Plant balled and burlapped trees now; if bare-rooted, wait until next month.

Quickest growing: Weeping willow, locust, tulip poplar, Bradford pear, Golden raintree.

For winter beauty:

Deciduous: Moraine locust, beech, Yoshino cherry, ginkgo, dogwood, hickory, maple, white oak, sourwood, sweet gum.

Evergreen: Magnolia glauca (sweet bay), magnolia grandiflora, cherry laurel, pine, hemlock, spruce, fir, Cunningham, cryptomeria.

FERTILIZERS

Use compost on garden beds. If no compost is available, broadcast lime and manure on soil at 2 week intervals.

INSECT AND DISEASE CONTROL

Moth balls on the perimeter of a garden bed repel rodents digging for grubs.

PLAN AHEAD

Order for Christmas giving.

BLOOMS

FLOWERS
Chrysanthemum
Cosmos
Rose
Snapdragon

SHRUBS
American Witchhazel
Camellia japonica
Camellia sasanqua

BERRIES
Aucuba
Dogwood
Euonymus
Holly
Ligustrum
Nandina
Pyracantha

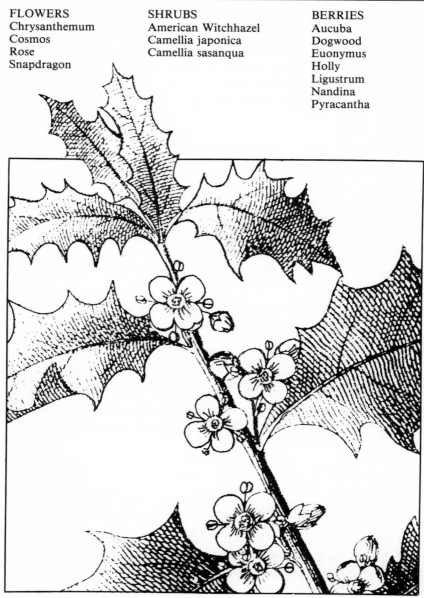

DECEMBER
THE MONTH FOR GIFTS FROM THE GARDEN

WEATHER AND SOIL

First lengthy freezing spells or early snow can be expected. (See January for instructions on care in cold weather.) Be sure to turn compost heap before it freezes.

FLOWERS

Annuals: In open weather, plant sweet peas.

Perennials: Last chance to plant tulips early in month.

Other late bulbs can be planted in open weather.

Continue planting roses.

Check bulbs in storage.

VEGETABLES

Harvest everything before hard freeze.

Onions easily withstand our winters.

Turnips, cabbage and collards will not survive below 10°.

SHRUBS

All types of shrubs can still be planted, if ground is not too frozen to work properly. Mulch all new plantings.

This is the best month to move old boxwood. Prune boxwood now only if necessary; otherwise wait until February.

TREES

Bare root trees can be planted now.

If any tree is more than 3″ in diameter, guy until spring, and wrap trunk. (See tree planting illustrations).

Native trees, which you've had your eye on in the woods, can be transplanted by mid-month. These should have been root-pruned in the spring and early summer.

LAWNS

Mow Rye grass at high notch on mower.

INSECT AND DISEASE CONTROL

A paste of wood ashes and water painted on tree trunks repels borers.

PLAN AHEAD

Order catalogues, check tools, start planning spring garden.

Send gift garden publications for Christmas presents.

BLOOMS

FLOWERS
Christmas Rose
Christmas Honeysuckle

SHRUBS
Camellia

BERRIES
Aucuba
Callicarpa
Citrus Trifoliata
Dogwood
Euonymus
Hawthorn

Holly
Ligustrum
Nandina
Pyracantha
Sumach

MISCELLANEOUS

Make winter bouquets of shrubs in fruit or evergreens with berries.

Make arrangements of your dried flowers. Use both of these as Christmas gifts, as well as flowering bowls of paperwhites and pots of forced bulbs.

Feed the birds.

CHAPTER II

LANDSCAPE DESIGN

Planning and planting for a house and lot is a challenge. The plan can reflect the owner's wish to keep expenses and maintenance down, and to emphasize all the best qualities of existing grades and trees.

FOUNDATION PLANTING

A landscape plan begins with "foundation planting" after satisfactory grading has been completed. Stand far enough back so the entire front of the house can be studied at one time. The door is the welcoming focal point of the entire plan. Avoid elements that will shatter this point. Overuse of "pine islands", walkways going in different directions, prominent car park areas and house trim colors detract from the focal point.

In choosing the "foundation planting" that will nestle the house to the grounds, keep in mind the ultimate heights and widths of shrubs and trees. With small sharp sticks, stake out groups of imaginary plants, or draw them as blobs on a simple sketch. Arrange them in groups, never in continuous unbroken lines. Leave spaces between groups where the house may be seen resting on the ground, and indicate strips of evergreen ground covers, or of brick or flagstone which should be laid flush to the ground for easier mowing. Plan tall shrubs at outer corners, mediums in the middle, and low plants grouped at the steps. They will stay that way if well chosen, requiring light pruning every other year. When pruning, remember that no shrub of its own free will, will ever grow egg-shaped, and no shrub grows with a flat top. Our area is rich in dwarfs which never grow over eighteen inches (such as Gumpo azaleas) and in superb tall broadleaf evergreens (such as Nellie Stevens holly, Cleyera, Camellia japonica, podocarpus) which will gladly reach ten, twelve, fourteen feet. Use a little quality mixed with plenty of space to balance a lovely house, and the plan will live forever.

THE PATIO

Plan for the patio, or outdoor terrace area. Depending on sun, grading and convenience, this space can be developed on the front, side or back of the house. This living area is rarely large enough, so on your list under "terrace", write "try out furniture". Literally carry enough tables and chairs outdoors to accommodate the family or the usual party, and arrange them in the area where the patio is to be built. Note that for every table and group of chairs there must be that same size space with nothing in it. Only then will you be able to move around with ease. Avoid narrow beds along house walls; flowers hate them because they are always bone dry, and people step in them. Take patio surfaces up to house walls, more space, less maintenance. Then use flowers in planters on rollers.

ENTRANCES AND EXITS

Do not forget to make a plan for the front walk before the builder's automatic narrow concrete strip appears. The minimum width for the walk should be four feet and the surface should blend with the front steps. In your plan, also list "garbage cans, air conditioning units and meters". Go carefully over the placing of each, and screen them. Then a last "don't": do not let the back door be designed in such a way that it is more available than the front door. Plan ahead for a beautiful, low maintenance, long-lasting home environment.

CHAPTER III

HOW TO PREPARE AND MAINTAIN
THE SOUTHEASTERN GARDEN

A green thumb is a dirty thumb.* The ability to cultivate a garden comes from working with plants. The majority of plants require only good soil, sun and one inch of water a week. The basic care and feeding of the garden includes soil preparation, planting, fertilizing, watering, and disease and pest control. With a few tools, a little time, and a dirty thumb a proud garden can be yours.

*The Garden Book, White Flower Farm, Litchfield, Connecticut

SOIL PREPARATION, FERTILIZERS, MULCH

The soil should be properly prepared before buying the first seed or plant. Plants will thrive and maintenance will be reduced if the soil has a good texture, the correct supplements, and the proper pH.

FERTILE SOIL

The texture of the soil is improved by adding organic matter. Organic matter, or humus, is any decayed plant or animal material. Humus turns hard, red clay into a soft workable garden soil that you will be proud to claim. You can make a compost pile with anything that would normally be discarded, such as wood shavings, ashes, barnyard manure, grass clippings or leaves. Allow these to decay for a year and then add to planting areas. Pine bark mulch and peat moss are commercially available, ready-to-use sources of humus.

SOIL SUPPLEMENTS

The Extension Service of the U.S. Department of Agriculture furnishes soil testing kits free-of-charge. They will analyze your sample and mail you an explanation of what your soil needs. Deficiencies in the soil are corrected by adding fertilizers.

Bagged and bottled chemical fertilizers contain three primary soil nutrients. The numbers on the label tell you the proportions of each nutrient; the higher the number, the greater the concentration of that nutrient. The first number indicates Nitrogen, the second, Phosphorus, and the third, Potash.

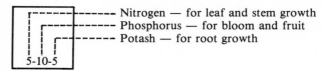

Nitrogen — for leaf and stem growth
Phosphorus — for bloom and fruit
Potash — for root growth
5-10-5

If the soil needs only one of the nutrients, you can purchase just that one. Use these with caution. If allowed to come in direct contact with the plant, severe burning will occur.

Nitrate of Soda: Immediate acting and a concentrated source of nitrogen for leaf and stem growth.

Super Phosphate: A concentrated source of phosphorous for blooming.

Muriate of Potash: Concentrated source of Potash for root growth.

Organic fertilizers are those taken from nature and are less likely to cause burning.

Bone Meal: 2-28-0, to promote bloom.

Cottonseed Meal: 6-2-1, for leaf growth and bloom.

Barnyard Manure: About 10-5-10, balanced nutrients.

Fish Emulsion: 5-2-0, for leaf growth and bloom.

pH is the measurement from 1 to 14 of the acidity and alkalinity of soil. 7 is neutral, lower numbers are more acid, higher numbers more alkaline. Southeastern soils are usually acid, from pH5 to pH6. Since some plants like azalea, camellia and holly prefer more acid soils, the soil test may suggest lowering the pH. Decayed pine needles and oak leaves are naturally acid or aluminum sulfate can be purchased and added to the soil. Grasses and some flowers, like Baby's Breath, prefer a more alkaline soil, so wood ashes or dolomitic lime can be added.

HOW TO PREPARE THE SOIL

You will need

1. Supplements recommended by the Extension Service soil test.
2. As much humus as possible.
3. A shovel and mattock for small areas.
4. A rototiller for large areas.
5. A soil rake.

Procedure for new planting areas

1. Chemically kill or dig out weedy growth.
2. Remove topsoil and set aside.
3. Remove soil to a depth of ten inches.
4. Mix soil supplements and humus with both piles of soil. When using a rototiller, the supplements are spread on the soil first, then tilled under.
5. Put topsoil mixture back first, then the subsoil mixture. Rake smooth and after a good rain settles the soil, it is ready to plant. Avoid walking on the newly worked soil as much as possible.

Results

1. Water will penetrate the soil easily.
2. Nutrients will be readily available for plant's use.
3. Soil can be worked earlier in the spring.
4. Plant growth will be optimum.

PROCEDURE FOR ESTABLISHED PLANTINGS

Nitrogen is quickly depleted by the long growing season in the Southeast, and should be added annually to lawns and plants. Blooming plants need a balanced fertilizer. It is important to follow the instructions on the product and to water well after application. Fertilizer is added in the Spring before new growth begins. There are two exceptions; azaleas should not be fertilized until after they bloom. Lawns and alkaline-loving plants should be limed in the fall, because lime is slow to act.

MULCH

The purpose of mulching, covering the soil area around plants, is to conserve moisture, inhibit weed growth, and give a finished appearance.

The choice of material should be in keeping with the landscape setting:

TYPE	CHARACTERISTICS
Black Plastic	Long lasting, weed free but only advised for commercial growers
Wheat Straw	For vegetable gardens, can be tilled under in the Fall
Wood Chips	Available free from tree service companies
Dried Grass Clippings	Readily available
Leaves	Readily available
Bark Nuggets or Chips	Packaged and easily transported
Pea Gravel	Lasts forever
Pine Straw	Author's choice

PLANTING, TRANSPLANTING AND GRUBBING OUT

Grubbing out and transplanting represent the opposite poles of feeling for a gardener. Grubbing out is removing a plant you do not want anymore. By vigorously attacking the roots with a mattock or shovel, you can be rid of a tired, old privet. Grubbing out is a suitable culmination to filing your income tax. Transplanting is moving a plant from one spot to another in hopes of saving it. Transplanting is a suitable culmination of hearing your stock has doubled. One requires unabandoned belligerence; the other demands optimistic persistence.

For success in transplanting, the new location must meet the plant's cultural requirements: sun or shade? moist or dry soil? adequate space to reach maturity? Perhaps a Magnolia grandiflora would look good by your brick terrace. Because a magnolia's roots grow rampantly near the surface, within twenty years your best friend had better be a brick mason.

WHEN TO TRANSPLANT

Dormancy is the rest period of the plant and the best time to make your move. For most plants, dormancy occurs between December and March or before new growth begins in the Spring. The only difference between planting and transplanting is that the nursery man does the "digging up".

DIGGING UP

The amount of root growth you remove from the plant determines how much you will have to prune it. If you chop away one-third of a Nandina's roots, then at least one-third of the canes should be removed. *(See drawing of root pruning.)*

A good root ball means digging out the plant with as much dirt left on as is possible. If you have to cut large roots stick a potato on them to retain moisture and speed root growth.

The plant is then lifted from the hole and the ball should be wrapped in a tarp or burlap. Burlap can stay on the root ball; plastic must be removed.

REPLANTING

The new hole should be dug so that the plant will be growing at its original soil level. The hole should be larger than the root ball or "dig a $5.00 hole for a $1.00 plant". Organic matter or humus, such as peat moss, pine bark mulch or well-decayed compost should be mixed with the soil. Half soil, half humus is ideal. Any fertilizer should be added only after the roots are covered, as a top dressing.

Watering is essential to force out any air pockets around the roots. Do this by pushing the hose down into the loose soil around the rootball. Any tree over four feet tall should be staked for a year in order to hold the tree upright in strong winds. The material used to tie the tree off must not cause girdling of the trunk. Girdling is a horticultural term for strangulation.

Finally, a layer of mulch such as pine straw is applied to retain moisture, inhibit weeds, and cover all the work you have done.

PLANTING A TREE

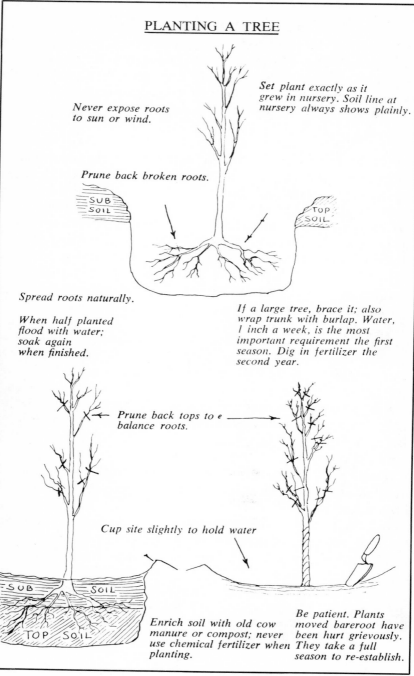

Set plant exactly as it grew in nursery. Soil line at nursery always shows plainly.

Never expose roots to sun or wind.

Prune back broken roots.

SUB SOIL

TOP SOIL

Spread roots naturally.

When half planted flood with water; soak again when finished.

If a large tree, brace it; also wrap trunk with burlap. Water, 1 inch a week, is the most important requirement the first season. Dig in fertilizer the second year.

Prune back tops to e balance roots.

Cup site slightly to hold water

SUB SOIL

TOP SOIL

Enrich soil with old cow manure or compost; never use chemical fertilizer when planting.

Be patient. Plants moved bareroot have been hurt grievously. They take a full season to re-establish.

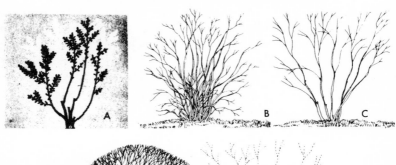

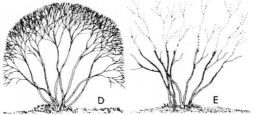

THE FUNDAMENTALS OF PRUNING

*For overgrown shrubs (Lilacs, Rhodos, etc.) take out two
big branches annually (A), otherwise shrubs will drown
in own sap. For twiggy shrubs (B) remove from base (C).
Crew cut (D) undesirable. To force twigginess at bottom,
prune as in (E) Yews should be pruned as growth starts.*

Root Pruning

*This schematic drawing shows how a
root system develops (lower right, in
and out of circle). The spade (be sure
to sharpen it with a file) should be
driven at an angle. Although the drawing shows a small deciduous tree be-
ing root-pruned, the same technique is
used for shrubs.*

WATERING

In the South on a torrid August day, sprinklers throw a cool mist over a parched lawn and it is the best time in a gardener's day. Homeowners are inclined to haphazardly water plants, probably because it's one of the easiest and most delightful gardening tasks. However, deep watering of lawns and plants enables them to sustain extremes in the weather, far better than an occasional light once over.

HOW MUCH TO WATER LAWNS

Set up several cans in the area that the sprinkler will cover. Check to see how long it takes to accumulate one inch of water in the cans. This tells you how long to water a lawn. One inch per week is enough.

HOW MUCH TO WATER PLANTS

Soaker hoses, running at a slow trickle with the holes down, are best for watering vegetables, shrubs and trees, because the foliage stays dry, and flowers are not beaten to death. To find out how long to water with soaker hoses, dig into the roots at thirty minute intervals. The soil should be wet to a depth of two inches for shallow rooted plants like tomatoes and azaleas, three inches for deeper rooted plants like raspberries and hollies, and four inches for trees.

WHEN TO WATER

The two critical times of year that plants need water are in the fall, to encourage deep rooting before cold weather, and in the hot dry summer to prevent wilting. The time of day to water a lawn is generally not important. Water when convenient.

But, if the number of plants you have is so great that watering by sprinklers is the only feasible method, the time of day is often extremely important. Zinnias, Phlox and Crape Myrtle should not be watered at nightfall because the leaves will mildew. If Hostas, Boxwood and Ferns are watered in direct sun, the foliage sunburns. If unsure about a particular plant, the safest time to water is early in the morning.

PEST AND DISEASE CONTROL

The best "medicine" for plants are these preventive measures:
1. Keep plants growing in a fertile soil.
2. Dispose of plants and debris that harbor pests.
3. Keep tools cleaned.
4. Inspect the roots and the top growth of new plants before purchasing.

Chemical eradication of pests and disease should be your last resort. This method can make you sick, can wipe out your neighbor's garden, and can do long-term damage to your environment. (See the calendar section of this book for safer alternatives.)

It is surprising that restrictions on toxic garden chemicals are so few. Make yourself read EVERY WORD on the label and follow directions exactly.

Chemicals come in three forms. Water soluble powders are the most economical for large areas, but are difficult to mix. For most gardeners, liquids and dusts are the easiest. For large garden areas, hose-end sprayers are the fastest. For restricted spaces, pressure sprayers in a canister are more versatile.

WHAT YOU WILL NEED

1. The correct chemical for your problem.
2. A sprayer with an adjustable nozzle.
3. A bottle of spreader-sticker to help the spray stay on the foliage.
4. For dusts, a large paint brush is a good applicator.

HOW TO SPRAY

1. Choose a day that is not windy.
2. When using systemic sprays, a face mask and covering for all exposed skin should be worn.
3. Never put herbicides in a sprayer used for anything else.
4. Do not mix different chemicals unless the label says it is safe.

5. Put several drops of spreader-sticker into sprayer.
6. Add measured amounts of chemical and water to sprayer.
7. Apply mixture in a steady stream to affected plants only, adjusting nozzle to cover the undersides of foliage as well as the tops.
8. Rinse all parts of the sprayer thoroughly. Store chemicals properly. Wash hands well.

INSECT PROBLEMS

The following chart identifies some of the most common problems facing gardeners in the south. Before using any of the products, be certain the plant you are treating is not mentioned in the DO NOT column on the product label.

VISIBLE SIGN	PLANT	TREATMENT
Leaves chewed, Scale on foliage	almost any plant	Dormant oil spray as a preventative in winter
Flower buds chewed by Rose Chafers	Roses, Peonies	Lindane, only as first buds appear
Leaves finely mottled by Red Spider	Dahlias, roses, azaleas & others	Malathion, weekly or Systemic insecticide
Many small, active insects — Aphids	almost any plant	Systemic insecticide
Branches or entire tree killed by Borers	fruit trees, dogwood	No cure known, use tree wound dressing on all pruning cuts as a preventative
Leaves eaten through in irregular patterns by Lace Bugs	many ornamentals agricultural crops	Malathion
Hundreds of nervous flying insects on foliage — White Flies	Indoor & Outdoor Ornamentals	Systemic insecticide
White map-like tracings on foliage — Leaf Miner	Boxwood, Columbine	Systemic insecticide
Skeletonized leaves and chewed flower petals — Japanese Beetles	Ornamentals Agricultural crops	Diazinon Carbaryl
Small plants chewed off at the soil line — Cut Worms	young annuals	Diazinon
Ants	Any plant	Malathion
Leaves swollen by leaf gall	azaleas	Zineb

VISIBLE SIGN	PLANT	TREATMENT
Cottony deposits on stems — Mealy Bugs	houseplants	Systemic insecticide
Small white spots on leaves — Leafhoppers	any plant	Diazinon or Carbaryl
Beetle Grubs, larvae in the ground	lawns and flower beds	Diazinon
Dark spots on foliage — Blackspot	Roses	Daconil
Gray cottony appearance to leaves or stem — Mildew	Roses, phlox, fruits, vegetables	Benomyl
Seedlings fall over & die Damping off	any seedlings	Dust seed with Semesan before sowing
Center of plant blackens, dies — Crown Rot	Begonias and some flowering perennials	Drench soil with Semesan solution
Dark, dead patches in lawn — Fungus	grasses in very wet weather	Daconil
Small toadstools in lawn — Fairy Ring	grasses in summer	Daconil
Yellow blotching or crinkled leaves — Virus	Geraniums, daffodils, lilies	Dig up and destroy, spray area with Diazinon

MISCELLANEOUS DISORDERS

VISIBLE SIGN	PLANT	TREATMENT
Crabgrass	in lawns	Pre-emergence herbicide in late winter
Slugs	Herbaceous plants	Slug bait
Yellowing between veins of leaves — Chlorosis	Acid loving plants	Chelated Iron
Soil disrupted; small plants uprooted — Rodents	any exposed soft soil area	moth balls around perimeter of the garden
Bark or foliage stripped — Deer or Rabbits	Young trees; tender foliage	Thiram
Nutgrass	in beds; lawns	Round-Up, only on the nutgrass

TOOLS

Purchase the best tools on the market if you do extensive gardening. Fertilizers and soils left on tools will rust them. Paint the tips of long handled tools a bright color to keep from losing them under a pile of leaves. The best time to assess your tools is in January, before you will need them. Have dull cutting blades sharpened, broken handles repaired, add clean oil, and put new spark plugs in engines.

THE BASIC GARDENING TOOLS

For cutting

Hand clippers, loppers, and a branch saw.

For digging

Trowel, a long-handled shovel with a rounded blade, a mattock, a digging fork, and a hoe or potato fork.

For hauling

Wheelbarrow and a tarp.

For cleaning up

Leaf rake, push broom, flatheaded shovel, a soil rake.

For watering

Hoses, soaker hoses, an adjustable nozzle, coupling repair kits and sprinklers.

For pest/disease control

A hand held spray bottle for individual plant treatment and a sprayer for large areas.

For grass

A lawn mower.

For your hands

Washable cotton gloves are best for daily use. Leather work gloves are also needed for protection from thorns and heavy duty jobs. Packaged handi-wipes are convenient supplies to keep in your tool box.

CHAPTER IV

WHAT TO PLANT AND HOW TO PLANT IT
IN THE SOUTHEAST

In planning the garden there are many choices. Garden varieties that grow well in the area known as the Southern Piedmont, are often excluded from garden books written for all of the United States. The Southern Piedmont is shown on the map on page 8. The following lists of plants were chosen because of their excellent characteristics. Either the foliage, bloom, or rate of growth is special and the plant does not create a large maintenance problem, or the plant is hardy and thrives in our short, cold winters as well as in our long, hot summers. Also included are some well-known plants that are questionably hardy, which, unless sited correctly on the property, may succumb to weather extremes. In each plant list, these plants are noted.

SOUTHERN LAWN GRASSES

The problem with growing a beautiful lawn in the Southeast is the climate. It is too cold for summer grasses to stay green all winter, and too hot for cool season grasses to stay green all summer. There is no one grass that is the best.

Your choice should be based on your needs, not your neighbors. If boys play ball on your lawn, wear-tolerance is important. If your design is formal, fine leaf texture is important. Establishing a lawn by vegetative means, sprigging or sodding, is much more costly than seed. The following chart grades southern grasses on these and other characteristics.

SOUTHERN LAWN GRASSES

SOUTHERN LAWN GRASSES	LEAF TEXTURE	HARDINESS: HOT, COLD, WEAR SUN, SHADE, DROUGHT	pH	GROWTH RATE	WATER & FERTILITY REQUIREMENTS	CUTTING HEIGHT	ESTABLISHED
COOL SEASON GRASSES							
Fescue	coarse	all good	5.5-7.5	high	medium	½"-1½"	seed
Kentucky Bluegrass	medium	all good except poor shade adaptation	6.0-7.0	med.	med.	1½"-3"	seed or vegetative
Rye, perennial	med.	all good	6.0-7.0	very high	med.	1"-1½"	seed
Rye, annual	coarse	good wear & shade, poor heat/cold hardiness	6.0-7.0	very high	med.	1"-2"	seed
WARM SEASON GRASSES							
Bermuda, common	med.	all good to excellent but poor shade adaptation	5.5-7.5	high	med. fert. low water	1½"-2½"	seed
Bermuda, hybrid	med.	all excellent but fair cold poor shade adaptation	5.5-7.5	high	high fert. low water	½"-1½"	vegetative
Zoysia	med. fine	all good but cold hardiness only fair	6.0-7.0	low	med. fert. low water	½"-1½"	vegetative
St. Augustine	coarse	med. wear, excellent heat and shade resistance, poor cold, fair drought.	6.5-7.5	med.	med.	1½"-2½"	vegetative
Centipede	coarse	poor wear, good shade & heat, fair cold & drought resistance	4.5-5.5	low	low fert. med. water	1"-1½"	seed or vegetative

furnished by U.S. Department of Agriculture

GROUND COVERS

Ground covers are perfect plants to introduce in areas where grass is difficult to maintain. Some ground covers should be used only in enormous bare areas. Their growth is so rampant that they will have to be continually cut back from neighboring plants: Polygonum reynoutria, ivy, and Bishop's Weed have a growth rate that is second only to kudzu!

HOW TO PLANT

Ground preparation for new ground covers is the same as for any plant. Plenty of humus is worked into the soil after weeds and stones are removed, then the area is raked smooth before planting. It is easier to spread the mulch first, then plant through it. The area should be watered weekly until the plants are established and growing well. Every spring before new growth begins, one of the organic fertilizers, like cottonseed meal, is broadcast over the area and watered well.

GROUND COVERS FOR SHADE:

NAME	CHARACTERISTICS
Arum italicum	White flowers, spring, red berries, summer; deciduous
Begonia evansiana	Pink flowers late summer, deciduous
Epimedium rubrum or sulphureum	Red or yellow flowers spring, semi-evergreen
Foam Flower (Tiarella cordifolia)	White flowers spring, evergreen
Galax	Glossy evergreen foliage
Lily-of-the-Valley (Convallaria)	White flowers, spring, deciduous
Pachysandra	White flowers spring, evergreen
Vinca Minor or Major	Blue or white flowers spring, evergreen
Wild Ginger (Asarum canadense)	For moist spots, deciduous

GROUND COVERS FOR SUN

NAME	CHARACTERISTIC
Juniper, Creeping	Evergreen 1 foot conifer
Sedum	Evergreen succulent

GROUND COVERS FOR SUN OR SEMI-SHADE

NAME	CHARACTERISTIC
Ajuga	Blue flowers, spring, evergreen
Geranium (true)	Blue, lavendar, or white flowers, summer, deciduous
Lamium	Variegated foliage, evergreen
Mondo Grass (Ophiopogon)	Blue berries, winter. Dense mats of evergreen
Monkey Grass (Liriope)	Purple or white flowers spikes late summer, evergreen
Wintercreeper (Euonymus)	Prolific spreader, evergreen

VINES

In nature vines scramble over other plants with great abandon. You do not have to own a trellis to have flowering vines. Use trees and larger shrubs for their support, or train them against a bare corner of the house, using masonry nails in brick or small screw eyes in wood.

THE PLANTING AND CARE OF VINES

Flowering vines are beautiful additions to mailboxes. Evergreen vines can be trained to disguise eyesores such as a cyclone fence. Like other plants, vines perform best when fertilized in late winter and kept well mulched. They will be spectacular if planted where they can mature naturally without constant pruning. Only large flowered Clematis need pruning, and they are cut back to eighteen inches in late winter.

The following vines need to be grown in full sun except where noted.

COMMON NAME	BOTANICAL NAME	CHARACTERISTICS
Banksia Rose	Rosa banksiae	yellow flowers, spring
Carolina Jessamine*	Gelsemium sempervirems	yellow flowers, spring
Cherokee Rose*	Rosa laevigate	white flowers, spring
Clematis armandi	Clematis armandi	white flowers, spring, evergreen for shade
Confederate Jasmine	Trachelospermum jasminoides	fragrant white flowers, summer, needs winter protection

COMMON NAME	BOTANICAL NAME	CHARACTERISTICS
Crossvine*	Bignonia capreolata	red or yellow spring flowers
Euonymus	Euonymus fortunei	white flowers, spring, red summer fruit, evergreen for sun or shade
Fig, Creeping	Ficus pumila	evergreen for shade, needs winter protection
Hydrangea, Climbing	Hydrangea petioloris	white flowers, summer
Muscadine Grape*	Vitis rotundifolia	edible fruit, summer
Ivy	Hedera helix	evergreen
Passion flower*	Passiflora caerula	lavendar & white flowers, summer
Silver Lace Vine	Polygonum auberti	white flowers, summer
Scuppernong Grape*	Vitis rotundifolia	edible summer fruit
Virginia Creeper*	Parthenocissus quinquefoil	red foliage, autumn
Trumpet Creeper*	Campsis grandiflora	red flowers, summer
Wisteria	Wisteria sinensis	purple or white flowers, spring

TREES

Trees provide beauty, shade, windbreaks, noise barriers, food and homes for animals. Yet their care is often neglected by homeowners.

PLANT CARE

The first year trees are planted, they should be watered weekly throughout the growing season, if there is no rain.

Late winter of the second year, trees should be fertilized. Remove the mulch. Apply one cupful of fertilizer per trunk diameter inch, scratching into the soil in a circle below the tips of the branches. The roots of a tree extend at least as far as the branches. Replace the mulch; water. Repeat watering every two weeks during the growing season, if there is no rain.

The third year and thereafter, fertilize annually and water only during extended drought.

Pruning trees to remove either dead wood or crossing branches, or to shape its growth should be done in late winter.

POPULAR TREES

COMMON NAME	BOTANICAL NAME	CHARACTERISTICS
Bald Cypress*	Taxodium distichum	Red bark, rapid grower
Bradford Pear	Pyrus calleryana Bradford	Rapid grower, spring flowering, fall foliage
Buckeye*	Aesculus	Shade, Spring flowering
Cherry, flowering	Prunus	Spring flowering, interesting branching
Crab	Malus	Spring flowering, messy when fruiting
Cucumber Tree*	Magnolia acuminata	Shade
Dogwood*	Cornus florida	Spring flowering, Fall foliage & berries
Fringe Tree*	Chionanthus virginica	Spring flowering
Golden Raintree	Koelreuteria	Summer flowering
Gordonia*	Franklinia altamaha	Summer flowering, Fall foliage
Hemlock*	Tsuga canadensis	Graceful evergreen for sun or shade
Hickory*	Carya	Fall foliage, nuts, shade

COMMON NAME	BOTANICAL NAME	CHARACTERISTICS
Holly, American*	Ilex opaca	Evergreen, red berries
Japanese Cedar	Cryptomeria japonica	Evergreen
Judas or Redbud*	Cercis canadensis	Spring flowering
Magnolia, Southern*	Magnolia grandiflora	Fragrant Summer flowering, evergreen, rapid grower
Maidenhair	Ginko bilboa	Fall foliage
Maple*	Acer rubrum	Fall foliage
Oak, Live*	Quercus virginiana	Long-lived
Oak, Water*	Quercus nigra	Faster growing of the two oaks
Persimmon*	Diospyros virginiana	Edible fruit, bark pattern is blocks
River Birch*	Betula nigra	Brown peeling bark
Silver Bell, Carolina*	Halesia carolina	Spring flowering
Snow Bell*	Halesia carolina	Spring flowering
Sourwood*	Oxydendrum arboreum	Fall foliage, fruit
Sycamore*	Platanus occidentalis	White bark, shade
Yaupon*	Ilex vomitoria	Evergreen, red berries
Yellowwood	Cladastris lutea	Spring flowering, Fall foliage, silver-gray bark

*Native to the Southeast

SHRUBS

The southeast has one of the largest collections of shrubs in the world, and is particularly famous for its abundant broad leaf evergreens. The temptation is to plant far too many varieties in one garden. The result is an unsightly jumble.

HOW TO DECIDE WHAT TO BUY

Shrubs have different foliage textures. Burford holly foliage has a bright sheen, and the Viburnums have dull crinkled leaves. Shapes vary from the weeping branches of Forsythia to the stately pyramid of Osmanthus. Leaf forms can be the delicate fern-like Nandina, or the defiant formality of Yucca. In choosing shrubs, consider how all of these differences will combine.

Since most shrubs are purchased in cans, do not hesitate to knock one out of the can at the nursery to check the roots. If the roots are in tight concentric circles and fill up the can, if the soil smells sour, or if one-third of the can is just loose soil, do not buy it.

PROTECTING AGAINST COLD DAMAGE

Plants that may be damaged or killed in an unusually cold winter are questionably hardy. They should be planted in a protected spot:
1. With evergreens between the plant and northerly winds
2. Next to a wall or house
3. Under taller trees
4. Do not plant them in an open, south facing exposure. On a mild day in midwinter the sun may warm the plant enough to break its dormancy. Then the next cold spell will kill the new growth.

If snow and ice burn or even defoliate evergreens, as in the winter of 1982, do not prune them until you see where the new growth begins in the spring. They may look dead, but have no dead wood at all.

The shrubs in the following lists that are questionably hardy in the northern area of the Southern Piedmont are

Camellia japonica, Gardenia, Loquat, and Tea-Olive.
The asterisk indicates native plants.

DECIDUOUS SHRUBS FOR BLOOMING

Winter Flowering

COMMON NAME	BOTANICAL NAME	COLOR
Apricot, Flowering	Prunus glandulosa	white, pink, red
Golden Bells	Forsythia	yellow
Honeysuckle, Winter	Lonicera fragrantissima	white
Jasmine, January	Jasminum nudiflorum	yellow
Service Berry*	Amelanchier	white
Witch Hazel	Hamamelis	yellow
Wintersweet	Chimonanthus praecox	yellow

Spring Flowering

Azalea, Wild*	Rhododendron	white, yellow, orange
Beauty Bush	Kolkwitzia amabilis	pink, yellow
Blackhaw, Southern*	Viburnum prunifolium	white
Fothergilla*	Fothergilla gardenii	white
Globe Flower	Kerria japonica	yellow
Mock Orange*	Philadelphus indorus	white
Plum, Flowering	Prunus triloba	pink
Pomegranage, Flowering	Punica granatum	orange
Rose Acacia*, Flowering	Robina hispida	rose
Snowball	Viburnum americana	white
Sweetshrub*	Calycanthus floridus	dark red
Viburnum*	Viburnum alnifolium	white

Summer Flowering

Butterfly Bush	Buddleia davidi	lilac
Chaste Tree	Vitex agnus-caste	blue
Crape Myrtle	Lagerstroemia indica	red, white, pink
Glory Bower	Clerodendron trichotomum	white
Hydrangea, Oakleaf*	Hydrangea quercifolia	white
Hydrangea, P.G.	Hydrangea paniculata grandiflora	white
Stewartia*	Stewartia Malachodendron	white

Fall Foliage Color

Fothergilla*	yellow, red
Forsythia	purple
Hydrangea, Oakleaf*	red
Blackhaw*	red
Witch Hazel	yellow

EVERGREEN SHRUBS

Low Growing, 1 ft. - 5 ft.

COMMON NAME	BOTANICAL NAME	Max. Height
Andromeda	Pieris japonica	5 ft.
Azalea, Gumpo	Rhododendron ssp.	18 in.
Azalea, Kurume	Rhododendron ssp.	5 ft.
Cape Jasmine	Gardenia jasminoides	4 ft.
Cotoneaster	Cotoneaster horizontalis	10 in.
Daphne	Daphne odora and burkwoodi	2 - 5 ft.
Juniper	Juniperus ssp.	6 in - 3 ft.
Laurel	Laurocerasus schipkaensis	5 ft.
Leucothe*	Leucothe cataesbaei	5 ft.
Skimmia	Skimmia japonica	5 ft.
Spanish Bayonet*	Yucca gloriosa	4 ft.
Viburnum	Viburnum suspensum	5 ft.

Medium Height, 5 ft. - 10 ft.

Aucuba, Japanese	Aucuba japonica	10 ft.
Camellia	C. japonica C. sasangua	8 - 10 ft.
Dwarf Hinoki Cypress	Chamaecyparis obtusa nana	8 ft.
Euonymus	Euonymus japonicus	15 ft.
Heavenly Bamboo	Nandina domestica	8 ft.
Holly Grape	Mahonia bealei	10 ft.
Osmanthus	Osmanthus fortunei	6 ft.
Plum Yew	Cephalotaxus drupacea	10 ft.

Tall, Over 10 ft.

Anise	Illicum anisatum	12 ft.
Boxwood	Buxes sempervirens	25 ft.
Cherry Laurel	Laurocerasus cardiniana	18 ft.
Cleyera	Eurya ochnacea	15 ft.
English laurel	Laurocerasus officinalis	20 ft.
Elaeagnus	Elaeagnus pungens	15 ft.
Firethorn	Pyracantha coccinea	20 ft.
Ligustrum	Ligustrum japonicum	12 ft.
Loquat	Eriobotyra japonica	20 ft.
Loropetalum	Loropetalum chinensis	12 ft.
Mountain Laurel	Kalmia latifolia	15 ft.
Osmanthus, Holly Leaf	Osmanthus aquifolium	20 ft.
Photinia	Photinia serrulata	40 ft.
Rhododendron*	Rho. catawbiense	18 ft.
Tea-Olive	Osmanthus fragrans	25 ft.
Tea Plant	Thea Bohea	20 ft.

SHRUBS OF SPECIAL INTEREST IN THE SOUTHEAST

HOLLIES

Hollies are very popular in the South and are widely used. They adapt themselves to quick changes in climate and grow equally well in sun and shadows. The family withstands cold with less damage and death than many of the broadleaf evergreens, and today these beautiful, hardy plants are more generously used as a family than any other on the market.

PLANTING

Under no circumstances should a holly be planted deeper than it was originally set; in fact, if anything, it should be planted slightly higher, thus allowing for the ground to settle a wee bit.

FAVORITE HOLLIES OF THE SOUTHEAST

NAME	CHARACTERISTICS	USE
Ilex opaca American holly	light green foliage, upright and slow, red berries	windbreaker & barrier
Ilex opaca Croonenburg	thicker, dark foliage, red berries	specimen or background tree
Ilex opaca Howardii	upright grower, dark green foliage, red berries	foundation planting & masses
Ilex Fosteri No. Two	slow, upright, small green leaves, red berries	prunes well, good for standard forms, hedges & masses
Ilex Burfordi	shiny green foliage, large red berries	barrier, hedge, espalier
Ilex Bufordi nana	slow growing, compact miniature	under low windows, accents in green gardens
Ilex latifolia	tall, heavy grower, leaves resemble magnolia	good specimen tree
Ilex Cherokee	pyramid type, small leaves, dark green foliage	responds well to pruning

NAME	CHARACTERISTICS	USE
Ilex crenata rotundifolia	good foliage, easily prunted	hedges, screens, masses
Ilex crenata convexa	sun or shadows, small curved shiny leaves, lacy texture	foundation planting, hedges, specimens
Ilex aquipernyi	brilliant, small leaves, heavily serrated, red berries	pyramidal
Ilex crenata compacta	compact growth	no pruning needed
Ilex crenata	spreading, low growing, medium green foliage	requires little pruning
Ilex crenata Helleri	small leaves, dwarf, sun or shadows	good subsitute for box-wood in edging beds
Ilex vomitoria nana	will stand more shade, narrow leaves	boon to long low house, to steps
Ilex cornuta rotunda	semi-dwarf, grows slowly, tight, dense branching	specimen, barrier and in masses

AZALEAS

The "show-off" plant of the south is the Azalea. The ever-green varieties have become so popular that cities schedule festivals to coincide with their blooming date. The deciduous varieties include native whites, yellows, oranges and reds found throughout the southeastern woods and the Ghent, Mollis and Knap Hill Hybrids which have a splendid range of brightly colored blooms.

HOW TO CULTIVATE

Azaleas look their best when grown in semi-shade, but they adapt to full sun. Because they have very shallow roots, they should be kept moist during hot, dry weather, and fertilized after they bloom each year. Pruning is necessary only to remove dead wood. If enough humus is used, azaleas can be planted any day of the year that the soil can be worked, though winter is the best time to move them.

Evergreen azaleas are easily propagated by rooting cuttings in mid-summer under a mist, or in a pot of sand enclosed in a plastic bag. Deciduous azaleas are propagated by air-layering from summer until early spring.

Evergreen Azaleas:

Southern Indian Hybrids are the tallest and fastest growing but the least hardy. In colder sections, they should be planted with other evergreen shrubs or with walls protecting them from northern winds. They have large single flowers. The most common varieties are:

NAME	CHARACTERISTIC	TIME OF BLOOM
Duc de Rohan	orange, red	early midseason
Fielder's White	White with faint chartreuse blotch	early midseason
Formosa	Violet-red	late midseason
George Lindley Taber	White	early midseason
Mrs. G.G. Gerbing	White	early midseason
President Clay	Red	early midseason

Kurume Hybrids:

Vary in height from tall to medium and are usually upright in growth habit. Flowers are single and are borne profusely in a wide range of colors. They are the best known variety. All bloom early mid-season.

NAME	CHARACTERISTIC
Coral Bells	Low growing, red flowers
Hinode-Giri	Medium height red flowers
Salmon Beauty	Medium height red flowers
Snow	tall, white with faint chartreuse blotch

Satsuki Hybrids

Satsuki (means fifth month) bloom later than other well known varieties, usually in May or June. They are not dwarf varieties, but they are slow growing to a height of five feet or more. Flower color on any one plant varies greatly.

NAME	CHARACTERISTIC
Banko	White lightly flushed with pink
Bene-Kirin	Double rose flower
Higasa	Large rose pink flower
Miyuno No Tsuki	White with green blotch and rose pink border

Macrantha Hybrids

are upright, of medium height and have excellent foliage. They bloom from early midseason to very late. In the trade, the two most often available are labeled either Macrantha Red or Macrantha Pink.

Gumpo

Are very low and slow growing, with flowers 1½ " to 2 " wide. They bloom in May and June.

White Gumpo	Single white flowers
Pink Gumpo	Pink flowers with deeper flecks.

Cover the entire blooming season for azaleas and provide a great variety of color and growth habit.

Commodore	Spreading growth to 4 feet, flowers scarlet with purple blotch in late April.
Copperman	Dense growth to 4 feet, rose flowers, mid-May.
Helen Close	Dense growth to 4 feet, flowers white with pale yellow blotch in early May.
Phoebe	Spreading growth to 4 feet, pink flowers in late April.

CAMELLIAS

Both Camellia sasanqua and Camellia japonica have been in the south since the mid-19th century. C. sasanqua is the hardier and more vigorous of the two. It can easily be espaliered, and its ultimate height is 8 feet or more.

HOW TO GROW CAMELLIAS:

Camellia sasanqua grows best in an acid soil, rich in humus and well-mulched. Once established, this plant is not too particular about the amount of moisture in the soil. It is more insect resistant, and sun tolerant than Camellia japonica.

Camellia japonica must be grown in shade or semi-shade. Soil must be acid (pH 4.0 - 5.0), friable, rich in humus, and moist. A three inch mulch is recommended. It must be planted at its original soil level, and even higher in sandy soils.

Camellias should be fertilized annually just after blooming. Dormant spray should be used annually to prevent scale and other insects. No pruning is needed except to remove dead wood.

HOW TO CHOOSE A VARIETY

The list of Camellia varieties would fill a small book. It is up to you to insist that your local nursery is selling varieties that are hardy in your area. You do not want the flower buds killed by a late cold snap. The farther north you live, the more protected the planting area should be.

Once you have chosen a hardy variety, ask your nurseryman to show you a picture. This should tell you the form and color of the flowers, and the growth habit of the plant.

CAMELLIA SASANSQUA

Has glossy leaves and white, pink, purple, red and variegated fall bloom.

CAMELLIA JAPONICA

Has duller leaves and blooms from fall to spring. The flower buds of the following are the most resistant to cold:

Betty Sheffield	Pink & white
Gov. Mouton	Red & white
Marchinoness of Salisbury	Red & white
Vedrine	Red
Waterloo (Ethlington White)	White

GIBBING CAMELLIAS

Gibbing the Camellia is done to increase the flower size by using gibberellic acid.

Flower buds form in late summer and early fall. Purchase gibberellic acid and store it in the refrigerator. It will keep for several years. Snap out the leaf bud growing next to the swollen flower bud, leaving a tiny cup on the stem. Put a drop of gibberellic acid in the cup. This will enlarge that bloom and also make it bloom earlier.

By removing the leaf bud, you have stopped the terminal growth at that point on the branch, so you will not want to gib every bud on the plant.

ROSES

If you are a rose enthusiast, join the local chapter of the American Rose Society to find out the best methods for rose care in your area, and study the twelve different varieties of roses to decide which is best for you.

PLANTING ROSES

Roses need some afternoon shade, but should not be planted close to a tree that will use up the water and fertilizers.

Plant roses in the middle of winter, when roses are really dormant.

Soil for roses should be fairly heavy, but well-drained. In sandy soil, add extra humus for water retention. Set graft one inch below soil line.

AFTERCARE

Keep mulched with 3 inches of manure.

Fertilize once a month during the growing season, and water well.

Water weekly if there is no rain, but never wet foliage in late afternoon, or black spot will attack.

Prune just as plants begin to break dormancy. Elmer's Glue is a good cane sealer. The amount of wood removed is much less than in northern sections of the country. Ask your botanical garden or garden center to show you how much to remove.

When cutting blooms, leave at least two complete leaves on the remaining cane.

Combination sprays made for roses are the most efficient way to combat pests and disease.

WILD FLOWERS AND FERNS

Unless a garden is extremely formal, with clipped hedges and a manicured lawn, the addition of ferns and wild flowers will quietly enhance any planting. In concrete urban areas, the naturalistic planting is a welcome relief. A small patch of Bluets in a sunny corner mentally whisks you away to the mountains. Outdoor steps, softened with a collection of ferns and Fairy Wand, transports you to a shady woodland stream.

Wild flowers will be a trouble-free, permanent addition to your garden if you duplicate the type of soil and sunlight conditions they enjoy in nature.

Mail-order nurseries offer good selections of native plants and seeds, so there is no need to rip them out of the woods. You could be digging up the last clump of an endangered species.

The following chart lists characteristics of some of the best wild flowers. It is noted if they need particular soil conditions.

WILD FLOWERS FOR SHADE

COMMON NAME BOTANICAL NAME	CHARACTERISTICS	HEIGHT & SOIL
FOR SHADE		
Arbutus, Trailing Epigaea repens	evergreen creeper, white flowers, edible red berries	
Baneberry, white Actaea alba	white flowers, spring, white berries on red stalks	rich soil 2 - 3 feet
Beardtongue Pentsemon canescens	purple or pink flowers, summer	dry soil 1 - 3 feet
Bugbane Cimicifuga americana	white flowers, summer	3 - 8 feet
Cardinal Flower Lobelia Cardinalis	red flowers, summer	2 - 4 feet damp site
Fairybells Disporum languinosum	yellow flowers, spring red fruit	8 - 24 inch damp site
Fairy Wand Chamaelirium luteum	white flowers, spring	1 - 4 feet moist, rich soil

COMMON NAME BOTANICAL NAME	CHARACTERISTICS	HEIGHT & SOIL
Foamflower Tiarella cordifolia	white flowers, spring	6 - 12 inches rich soil
Galax Galax rotundifolia	evergreen, white flowers, spring	1 - 2½ feet
Goatsbeard, False Astilbe biternata	white flowers, summer	2 - 6 feet
Iris, Crested Dwarf Iris cristata	blue flowers, spring	4 - 9 inches
Iris, Vernal Iris verna	evergreen, fragrant blue flowers, spring	4 - 9 inches
Lady's Slipper Cypripedium acaule	pink flowers, spring	6 - 15 inches
Oconee Bells Shortia galacifolia	rare evergreen creeper white flowers, spring	damp site
Orchid, Yellow Fringed Habenaria ciliaris	yellow flowers, summer	1 - 2½ feet
Orchid, Snowy Orchis spectabilis	white and lavendar flowers, spring	5 - 12 inches damp site
Phacelia, Fringed Phacelia fimbriata	blue lavendar, or white flowers, spring	8 - 16 inches
Spiderwort Tradescantia virginiana	violet flowers, spring	8 - 24 inches
Solomon's Seal Polygonatum cummutatum	white flowers, summer blue fruit	2 - 5 feet
Toadshade Trillium luteum	yellow flowers, spring	4 - 12 inch rich soil
Valerian, Greek Polemonium reptans	blue flowers, spring	1 - 1½ feet rich soil
Wake-Robin, green Trillium viride	green flowers, spring	4 - 12 inches rich soil
Wild Ginger Asarum arifolium	evergreen, greenish-purple flowers, edible root	6 - 12 inches
Wintergreen Gaultheria procumbens	evergreen, creeper, white flowers, spring, red edible berries	

77

WILD FLOWERS FOR SUN OR SHADE

COMMON NAME BOTANICAL NAME	CHARACTERISTICS	HEIGHT & SOIL
FOR SUN OR SHADE		
Azalea, Flame Rhododendron calendulaceum	orange, red, or yellow flowers, spring	15 feet
Columbine, Wild Aquilegia canadensis	yellow and red flowers, spring	1 - 2 feet
Dogtooth Violet Erythronium americanum	yellow flowers, spring	4 - 10 inches rich soil
Hepatica Hepatica americana	blue, pink or white flowers, spring	4 - 6 inches dry site
Lobelia, Great Lobelia siphlitica	blue flowers, fall	1 - 5 feet rich moist soil
Phlox, Wild Blue Phlox stolonifera	purple flowers, spring	4 - 8 inches rich soil
Rosebay, Mountain Rhododendron catawbiense	evergreen, rose or purple flowers, summer	3 - 20 feet

WILD FLOWERS FOR SUN

COMMON NAME BOTANICAL NAME	CHARACTERISTICS	HEIGHT & SOIL
FOR SUN		
Aaron's Rod Thermopsis caroliniana	yellow flowers, spring	3 - 5 feet rich soil
Bird-foot Violet Viola pedata	blue flowers, spring	4 - 10 inches
Bluets Houstonia caerula	blue flowers, spring	6 - 8 inches
Butterfly Weed Asclepias tuberosa	orange flowers, summer	1 - 2½ feet dry site
Evening Primrose Oenothera speciosa	pink or white flowers, summer	8 - 24 inches drought resistant
Fire Pink Silene virginica	red flowers spring	6 - 24 inches insect trap
Harebell, Southern Campanula divaricata	white or lavendar flowers, summer	6 - 20 inches
Pitcher Plant Sarrancenia leucophylla	red flowers, spring	2 - 3 feet bog plant, insectivorous
Queen Anne's Lace Daucus carota	white flowers, summer	1 - 3 feet dry site

COMMON NAME BOTANICAL NAME	CHARACTERISTICS	HEIGHT & SOIL
Shooting Star Dodecatheon meadia	rose, lilac or white flowers, spring	8 - 20 inches
Smartweed Polygonum pensylvanicum	pink flowers, summer	1 - 6 feet
Tickseed, Greater Coreopsis major	yellow flowers, summer	1 - 2 feet
Turkscap Lily Lilium superbum	orange-red flowers, summer	8 feet
Verbena, Stiff Verbena rigida	pink flowers, summer	6 - 18 inches dry site
Yellow-Eyed Grass Xyris iridifolia	yellow flowers, summer	2 - 3 feet damp site

FERNS

Evergreen Ferns

COMMON NAME, BOTANICAL NAME	HEIGHT
Christmas Fern Polystichum acrostichoides	9-18 inches
Ebony Spleenwort Asplenium platyneuron	1-2 feet
Leather Wood Fern Dryopteris marginalis	1-2 feet
Polypody, Common Polypodium vulgare	6-18 inches
Resurrection Fern Polypodium polypodioides	6 inches
Toothed Wood Fern Dryopteris marginalis	1-2 feet

Deciduous Ferns

COMMON NAME, BOTANICAL NAME	HEIGHT
Bracken Fern Pteridium aquilinum	2-3 feet
Cinnamon Fern Osmunda cinnamomea	4-5 feet
Goldie's Fern Dryopteris goldiena	4-5 feet
Maidenhair Fern Adiantum pedatum	12-18 inches
Narrow Leaf Spleenwort Athyrium pynocarpon	3-4 feet

BULBOUS FLOWERS

Almost all Southeastern gardens look liveliest in the Spring. After the Winter months it is a joy to see the garden break out in a riot of Tulips, Daffodils, and early blooming perennials.

Summer blazes in so early after the fine show of Peonies, Iris and other spring favorites, then we depend on annuals to color the space of the spent perennials until the Dahlias and Chrysanthemums come in.

But there are many summer flowering bulbs that will color the midsummer months.

THE ADVANTAGES OF BULBS

1. Easier to plant than seed.
2. Once planted, most of them last forever.
3. Strong foliage that flourishes in our summer heat.
4. Flower shapes relieve the monotony of the daisy-shaped summer standbys.
5. Take up less room in the garden than the rank perennials of summer.

CULTURE

1. Plant in fall or spring.
2. Fertilize after blooming to nourish the bulb.
3. Remove spent flower head unless seed formation is desired.
4. Mulch in the winter.

BULBS

Camassia

3- or 4-foot spikes of blue starry flowers. They bloom early in the summer, and in Virginia they are naturalized.

Crinum Lily

Blooms from June till fall if several varieties are planted. The pale flesh colored ones seem to do as well here as the white. Amaryllis proper grows beautifully outdoors in South Georgia and Florida.

Gladioli

The Primulinius Hybrids have lovely colors, graceful stems and smaller spikes than the huge, stiff show stalks of the parent type, and have three or four stalks of bloom to each bulb.

Hemerocallis or Day Liles

Many superb varieties easily grown by gardeners throughout the entire southeast, ranging from pale yellow, apricot, pink to deep mahogany, and should be used more often in large masses.

Hostas or Plantain Lilies

Prefer semi-shade but behave equally well in the sun. Foliage makes beautiful clumps of rich, shiny green or variegated green and yellow. The spikes of lavender or white lily flowers come with abundance once they are established. White ones are fragrant.

Hyacinthus Candicans

Bulb with four-foot stalks of drooping white bell-shaped flowers that are fragrant.

Iris

First things planned to succeed the Tulips. Combining Bearded, Siberian and Spuria give six weeks of bloom.

Ismenes or Peruvian Daffodils

Easy as onions to grow and take up no more space. They have big, white, lily-shaped, fragrant flowers with foliage and stalk like Amaryllis.

Ixias or Corn Lilies

Somewhat like Montbretias in shape and size but come in lilac and pink and white as well as yellow. Bloom in early June.

Montbretias

Are persistent bulbs in scarlet, orange and yellows, bloom in June and sometimes again in the fall.

Tigridias

Exciting-looking little spotted flowers in bright colors on slender stems. Like dry sandy soil and sunshine.

Tritoma or Red Hot Poker

Splendid for the back of a border. Make fine tropical accents with their four foot spears of orange and scarlet bloom in mid-summer.

Tuberoses

Single Mexican is more graceful than the double ones that are better known. They and Gladioli bloom till late fall if planted in succession.

Zephyranthes or Fairy Lilies

White or pale pink, do as well in the garden as in the woods where they are native.

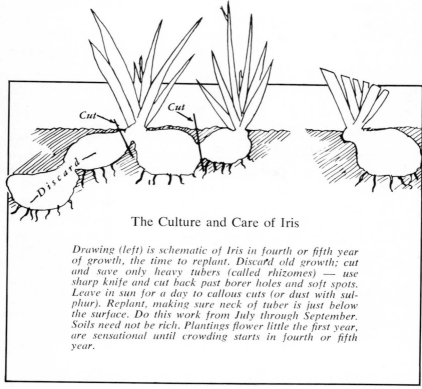

The Culture and Care of Iris

Drawing (left) is schematic of Iris in fourth or fifth year of growth, the time to replant. Discard old growth; cut and save only heavy tubers (called rhizomes) — use sharp knife and cut back past borer holes and soft spots. Leave in sun for a day to callous cuts (or dust with sulphur). Replant, making sure neck of tuber is just below the surface. Do this work from July through September. Soils need not be rich. Plantings flower little the first year, are sensational until crowding starts in fourth or fifth year.

THE FLOWER BORDER

A flower border is a collection of plants that bloom for several weeks, or throughout the growing season. The border is usually incorporated into another part of the landscape, or: against a wall, within a hedged line, or in front of tall shrubs. The easiest border consists of a mass of one variety for a single season of bloom. A border with a long succession of bloom is a challenge.

THE PLAN

1. Plot out the dimensions of the area you have chosen on graph paper.
2. Know the space needed for plants you will use.
3. Include something evergreen in order to have some winter interest.
4. Vary the shapes of flowers and the textures of foliage. Consider height, color, texture, and blooming time.
5. Be sure color combinations are pleasing.
6. Plant at least three of each variety for a good show.
7. Avoid plants that will spread rampantly and take over their neighbors.
8. Plant taller varieties in the back and middle of the border.
9. Include only plants that have similiar growing requirements.
10. To visually tie all of the elements together have either an evergreen bordering the area, a graduation of one color throughout, or a repetition of one variety in several spaces.
11. Though perennial varieties form the backbone of the border, the longest succession of bloom is possible by mixing in annuals.

ANNUALS

Annuals grow from seed, bloom and die in one year. There are three types of annuals: Hardy annuals, half-hardy annuals, and tender annuals.

Hardy Annuals

The seed requires cool soil to germinate, and are usually sown where they are to grow, because they resent transplanting. They can be sown in February or earlier if the soil was prepared in the fall.

Although hardy annuals burn out in the summer, the following are worthy because they bloom so early in the spring and often reseed themselves for more blooms the next spring. Be sure the seed packet says hardy annual, since many of these are also the names of perennials.

Alyssum	Lobularia maritima
Baby Blue Eyes	Nemophilia
Bachelor's Button	Centaruea cyanus
Forget-me-not	Anchusa capensis
Larkspur	Delphinium ajacis
Lobelia	Lobelia erinus
Love-in-a-mist	Nigella damascena
Pot Marigold	Calendula
Shirley Poppy	Papaver rhoeas
Sweet Pea	Lathyrus odoratus

Half-Hardy Annuals

These seeds should be sown inside in late winter or early spring for a longer blooming season. They are planted in the garden after the last frost date.

Browallia	
Celosia	
Cleome	
Flowering Tobacco	Nicotiana
Geranium	Pelargonium
Impatiens	
Nemesia	
Pepper, Ornamental	Capsicum annua
Periwinkle	Vinca rosea
Plumbago	
Snapdragon	Antirrhinum
Touch-me-not	Balsam
Wishbone Flower	Torenia

Tender Annuals

Tender annuals are best sown where they are to grow after the danger of frost is past. Some will survive transplanting from pots, packs, or flats if they are well developed.

Ageratum	
Aster	Callistephus chinensis
Cosmos	
Coleus	
Heliotrope	
Marigold	Tagetes
Morning Glory	Ipomoea
Nasturtium	
Petunia	
Scarlet Sage	Salvia
Stock	
Sunflower	Helianthus
Verbena	Vervain
Zinnia	

BIENNIALS

Biennials produce foliage the first year from seed and bloom the second year; they then die and often reseed themselves. They can be sown in spring or summer.

English Daisy	Bellis
Wallflower	Cheiranthus
Foxglove	Digitalis
Forget-me-not	Myosotis
Mullein	Verbascum

PERENNIALS

Perennials produce foliage the first year from seed and bloom for many years. The clumps increase in size each year. Some old favorites have been omitted (such as Lupine and Delphinium) that perform best where summers are cooler. Try them only if you have a cool spot in your garden. The recent increase in demand for perennials has encouraged nurseries to carry some of the best varieties. However, many of the following must be obtained by mail or from a friend. A variety name is given when it is superior to all others of that flower.

Achillea filipendulina
Achillea ptarmica — "The Pearl"
Anthemis
Asclepias — Butterfly weed
Aster x frikartii — Michaelmas daisy
Belamcanda — Blackberry lily
Chrysanthemum maimum — Shasta daisy
Chrysanthemum nipponicum — Oxeye daisy
Coreopsis — Tickseed
Dianthus barbatus — Sweet William
Dicentra spectabilis "Luxuriant" — Bleeding heart
Echinops — Globe Thistle
Epimedium — Bishop's hat
Geranium — Crane's bill
Geum chiloense
Helleborus — Christmas, Lenten rose
Hemerocallis — Daylily
Heuchera sanguinea — coral bells
Hosta — Plantain Lily or Funkia
Iris
Kniphofia — Red hot poker
Lychnis
Mertensia virginica — Virginia bluebells
Platycodon grandiflora
Rudbeckia — Black-eyed Susan
Salvia "Victoria" (blue)
Sedum
Solidago — Goldenrod
Stokesia laevis — Stokes aster
Thalictrum — Meadow rue
Veronica — Speedwell

CUT FLOWERS

The term cutting garden is again in vogue. In its nineteenth century context, it meant growing flowers in rows, somewhere far removed from the house. Today's cutting garden usually means a well-designed flower border near the house. Enough of each flower variety is grown for cutting and for garden display.

EQUIPMENT

Sharp knife or clippers; dull ones smash the capillaries in the stem. A bucket of warm water to carry to the flower bed. If you get the stems immediately in the water, it prevents wilting.

Oasis is the modern miracle that makes anyone adept at arranging flowers. Saturate it with water before putting it in the vase.

WHEN TO CUT

The best time to cut is late afternoon. Plants make their food supply during the day and that prolongs the life of the flower. The bucket of flowers should be placed in a cool, shady, wind-free spot overnight. This procedure makes the leaves and stems crisp as they fill with water. Keep flowers in water in the refrigerator for extended storage. To transport flowers, place them with ice in a cooler.

HOW TO CUT

Most flowers should be cut when they are half opened. Cut stems on a slant to expose more surface to water. Cut just above a leaf node for the sake of the plant. Remove all foliage that will be below the water except on roses and carnations. A teaspoon of sugar in a quart of water prolongs the life of cut flowers, and bits of charcoal keep the water smelling sweet.

HOW TO KEEP CUT FLOWERS FRESH LONGER

In General

1. Split the ends of woody stems.
2. Place hairy stems in hot water.
3. Sear oozy stems over a flame.
4. Recut hollow stems underwater.

Specifically

1. Marigold, snapdragon, sweetpea — recut stems underwater.
2. Campanula, chrysanthemum, daffodil, maidenhair fern, morning glory, helleborus, poppy, poinsetta, and wisteria — sear the stem.
3. Zinnias and Mock-Orange — remove all of the foliage.
4. Gardenia and Camellia — enclose in a box of wet paper overnight, or mist with cold water.
5. Daffodil, calla lily, zinnia, violet, and ivy — soak first in deep water.
6. Tulip, peony, and rose can be delayed in opening and transported safely if the flower bud is wrapped in plastic wrap.
7. Azalea, hydrangea, snapdragon, and other acid-loving plants benefit from a little vinegar in the water.

DRIED PLANT MATERIAL

Some plants, which are cut when green and brought into the house (for permanent arrangements), will dry naturally.

NATURAL DRYING

Magnolia grandiflora

Leaves become a warm brown without falling off the stem.

Aspidistra

Can be curled and pinned while still green for an abstract arrangement that dries to a rich brown.

Echinacea, Echinops, and Prairie Coneflower

Have large centers that retain their shape for years.

Japanese Bamboo

Delicate, rose-colored flowers hold their color for years, and hair spray keeps them from shattering.

Okra Pods

Dry on the stalk to a striped white and dark brown.

Nuts, cones and berries

Spread on newspaper to dry, can be used for Christmas decorations.

Silica Gel Procedure

Used to preserve the colors in flowers and foliage. Spread a layer of Silica Gel in an airtight container. Flowers must not be wet or the silica gel will stick to them. Cut stems off flowers and place heads face up. Sprinkle a layer of silica gel to cover them. Continue until container is full. Close container and check it in two days to see if flowers are crisp. Store flowers in another air tight container in the dark until ready to use for arranging, framing or potpourri.

All of the composite flower shapes like chrysanthemum and asters dry well with this method.

Others to try are:

Ageratum	Narcissus	Tulip
Coleus	Rose	Violet
Daylily	Snapdragon	Wallflower
Foxglove	Stock	

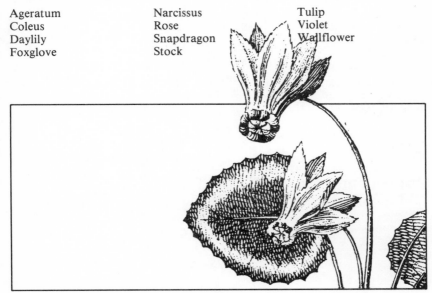

VEGETABLES

Once you have tasted the difference between your own freshly harvested fruits and vegetables and those from the market, "growing your own" will become an obsession. Even apartment dwellers can grow a cherry tomato in a wax milk carton. The brave homeowner will carve a hole in his front lawn for a vegetable garden if that is the only sun.

We are blessed in the Southeast with having an extended growing season that enables us to have three separate crops from one plot of ground. Even if you only plant a summer garden, a plot 74 ' × 74 ' that is well cared for will supply a family of four with fresh vegetables all summer.

CHOOSING THE SITE

1. Good soil with good drainage
2. Full sunlight
3. Access to water
4. A 2-4″ mulch between rows

FALL AND WINTER PLANTINGS

CROPS	DATE TO SOW
Asparagus	Nov. - March 15
Cabbage	Aug. 15 - Oct. 1
Lettuce, Bibb	Sept. - March 1
Mustard Greens	Sept. - April 1
Okra	Sept. - Oct. 1
Onion	Sept. - March 15
Peas, Garden or Snow	Jan. 15 - Feb. 15
Potatoes, Irish	Jan. 15 - March 1
Radish	Sept. - Oct. 15 & Jan. 15 - April 1
Spinach	Sept. - Oct. 15 & Jan. 15 - March 1
Turnip	Aug. - Sept. 15 & Jan. 15 - April 1

SPRING PLANTINGS

CROPS	DATE TO SOW
Beans, Bush & Pole	April 1 - May 1
Beans, Lima	April 1 - June 1
Beets	Feb. 15 - April 1

CROPS	DATE TO SOW
Broccoli	Feb. 15 - March 15
Cabbage	Jan. 15 - March 15
Cantaloupe	March 25 - April 20
Carrot	Jan. 15 - March 20
Cauliflower	March 1 - April 1
Collards	Feb. 1 - March 10
Corn	March 15 - June 1
Cucumber	April 1 - May 15
Eggplant	April 1 - May 15
Okra	April 1 - June 1
Onion	Jan. 1 - March 15
Peas, Southern	April - August
Pepper, Bell	April 1 - June 1
Potatoes, Sweet	April 15 - June 15
Squash, Summer	April 1 - May 15
Squash, Winter	April - August
Tomato	March 25 - May 1
Watermelon	March 20 - May 1

SUMMER PLANTINGS

CROPS	DATE TO SOW
Beans, Bush	July 15 - Aug. 20
Beans, Pole	July 15 - Aug. 10
Beans, Lima	July 10 - Aug. 1
Beets	Aug. 1 - Sept. 20
Broccoli	Aug. 1 - Sept. 1
Carrot	Aug. 20 - Sept. 15
Cauliflower	Aug. 1 - Sept. 1
Collards	Aug. 1 - Sept. 1
Cucumber	Aug. 1 - Sept. 1
Eggplant	July 10 - 25
Potato, Irish	Aug. 1 - Aug. 15
Squash, Summer	Aug. 1 - 20
Tomato	July 1 - Aug. 10

*These dates are furnished by the Cooperative Extension of the University of Georgia. Plantings in the Southeast that are north of Macon, Georgia, should be about two weeks later in the spring and earlier in the fall. Plantings south of Macon can be made about two weeks earlier in the spring and somewhat later in the fall.

HERBS

Herbs add spice to your garden. Grow "parsley, sage, rosemary and thyme"* along with mint, basil and most all of the popular herbs.

HOW TO PLANT

A small garden (6 ' × 8 ') will supply a large kitchen.

Prepare the soil as you would for vegetables. Loosen the soil for a depth of 10 inches and turn it. Sand may be needed in clay-like soil to make it airy and friable. Enrich the soil before planting with bone meal and humus. Herbs need full sun and good drainage.

*Simon and Garfunkel, "Scarborough Fair"

ANNUALS

NAME & HEIGHT	PLANT	NOTES
Anise 2 ft.	May 9 inches apart	seeds flavor cakes, bread, soups, stews
Basil 6-15 inches	after frost 15 inches apart	green or dry leaves season fish, and Italian sauce
Chervil (biennial)	rich, moist soil ½ day shade	flavor soup, salad one lettuce
Dill 23-36 inches	early spring, no transplant, thin and use	flavor pickles, vinegar, salad, soup, sauce
Parsley (biennial) 6-8 inches	soak seeds overnight to speed germination, rich soil, part shade, can transplant	garnish, flavor, breath freshener
Sweet Marjoram 8-10 inches	after frost, soak before planting, well-drained soil, full sun	dried or fresh season, soup, salad, vegetables

PERENNIAL HERBS

NAME	USE	CULTURE
Chives	oniony, cut leaves used to season salads, vegetables and cheese	easy growing, dig up and divide every 2-3 years
Garden Sage	dried leaves season sausage, salad dressing	plant 18″ apart, harvest July & August, dry leaves on screen
Garden Thyme	leaves used to flavor soups, salads, and sauces, meat and poultry, good in house	plant seed, self-sowing, keep well clipped
Mint (curly, apple, orange, pepper and spearmint)	leaves flavor beverages, vinegar, garnish	some shade, confine to prevent root spread
Rosemary	season soup, lamb, good in house	grow 14″, slow growing, full sun
Tarragon	flavoring for pickles, vinegar, chicken	partial shade, divide every year, space 2 ft. apart

GLOSSARY

FOR THE WORKING GARDENER

Air layering

propagation by rooting a stem while it is still on the plant.

Annuals

plants that live for only one growing season.

Biennials

plants that complete the life cycle in two years, flowering and fruiting the second year (beets, Sweet William, etc.)

Cold frame

a structure consisting of a wooden frame and a glass top, used for protecting young plants from the cold.

Compost

a collection of leaves, hay, weeds, and vegetable matter that is layered with soil and left to decay for about a year, at which time it is first rate fertilizer (humus).

Crown

the part of the plant, usually at the ground level, between the root and the stem.

Culture

gardening practice for the care and the raising of plants.

Cut back

see pruning

Cutting

a root, stem or leaf cut from a plant for rooting in order to create a new plant.

Deciduous

woody plants that drop leaves annually (ferns, maples, etc.)

Dormant

temporarily inactive, prefered time for planting.

Drainage

cultivation of soil to allow liquid to filter slowly through the soil instead of it holding water.

Evergreen

plants with foliage that persists and remains green throughout the year.

Espalier

training of trees or vines to grow in formal, two dimensional forms against a wall or fence.

Force

to cause plants to grow at increased rate by artificial means: force quince to bloom early by placing a cutting in water indoors.

Fertilize

feeding the plants. See Chapter III.

Flats

shallow box used for starting seeds.

Friable

refers to the soil's physical condition: damp soil that crumbles easily in the hand; clay-like southern soil may need sand added to make it friable.

Graft

propagation by bringing together the growing parts of two plants to grow as one.

Hardiness zones

refers to plant's ability to withstand cold, heat, wind, humidity or altitudes and to survive. There are 10 zones determined by the U.S. Department of Agriculture.

Heaving

bulging out of ground after hard freeze; danger of exposing roots.

Herbaceous

grass-like quality of foliage.

Humus

brown or black organic substance consisting of partially or wholly decayed vegetable matter that provides nutrients for plants, and increases the ability of soil to retain water.

Irrigation

see water.

Lime

a calcium compound for improving crops grown in soil that is deficient in lime.

Mulch

protective covering placed around plants to prevent evaporation of moisture, freezing of roots, and weeds.

Manure

animal feces used for fertilizer because of the humus it contains. Manure must be well rotted or composted before using or it will burn the plants.

Manure tea

liquid fertilizer made by dissolving manure in water.

Ornamentals

plants that are grown for use other than eating.

Peat

highly organic soil.

Perennials

plants that have a life span of more than two seasons (Iris, Chrysanthemum).

pH

measure of the soil's sweet or sour, alkaline or acid characteristics.

Pinching back

the act of nipping off stems, foliage in order to induce heavy bloom.

Propagate

to cause a plant (or animal) to multiply.

Prune

to cut back the plant in order to get the best form and show off flowers from a tree or shrub.

"Put to bed"

bury plants for protection from the cold.

Shade

the degree of light without direct sunlight. Light is necessary for even the most shade-loving plants.

Sow

to scatter seed for the growth of a plant.

Thin

to remove shoots to prevent crowding and allow the remaining shoots to develop strong stalks.

Top dress

to apply fertilizer on top of the soil.

Top soil

the fertile soil in which plants grow. Humus mixed with mineral soil.

Winter over

to prepare a plant by wrapping, shielding, or mulching so that it will be protected through the winter freeze.